the tiny kitchen
COOKBOOK

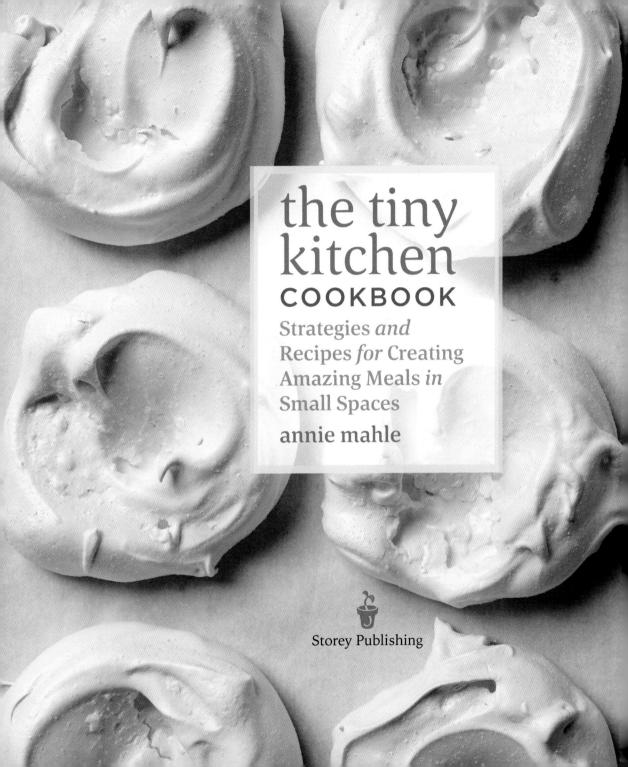

the tiny kitchen

COOKBOOK

Strategies *and* Recipes *for* Creating Amazing Meals *in* Small Spaces

annie mahle

Storey Publishing

The mission of Storey Publishing is to serve our customers by
publishing practical information that encourages
personal independence in harmony with the environment.

EDITED BY Carleen Madigan, Hannah Fries, and
Emily Spiegelman
BOOK DESIGN BY Jennifer Muller and Carolyn Eckert
ART DIRECTION BY Carolyn Eckert
TEXT PRODUCTION BY Jennifer Jepson Smith
INDEXED BY Samantha Miller

COVER AND INTERIOR PHOTOGRAPHY BY
© Kristin Teig
ADDITIONAL PHOTOGRAPHY BY © Ben Krebs, 10,
11, 29; © Davide Illini/Stocksy, 37; Mars Vilaubi
© Storey Publishing, LLC, 17 (m. & b.), 20 (t. & b.),
27 (l.), 31, 76 (t.l.)
FOOD STYLING BY Catrine Kelty

TEXT © 2021 BY ANNIE MAHLE

Storey books are available at special discounts
when purchased in bulk for premiums and sales
promotions as well as for fund-raising or educational use. Special editions or book excerpts can
also be created to specification. For details, please
call 800-827-8673, or send an email to sales@
storey.com.

STOREY PUBLISHING
210 MASS MoCA Way
North Adams, MA 01247
storey.com

Printed in China through World Print
10 9 8 7 6 5 4 3 2 1

Library of Congress Cataloging-in-Publication Data
on file

To those who love to cook and to the ones they nourish.
And to my extended Riggin *family—*
every one of you is a part of these pages and this food.

Contents

LOVE YOUR KITCHEN
(NOT THEIRS)

This book is about strategies for cooking delicious meals from scratch in tiny kitchens— creating big flavors in small spaces. No matter whether you live in a small apartment, tiny house, RV, boat, or college dorm, space in the kitchen is nearly always at a premium. Some of our kitchens are much smaller than others, but most of us could stand to be smarter about the space we have. After all, it's a rare one of us who has miles of counter space and gobs of storage at our disposal. Even in the smallest of kitchens, making delicious and healthy food is a goal easily within reach. Small spaces simply require that we be largely organized.

No matter the size of your kitchen, there are always moments when you'll wish for extra counter space or another cupboard. It's just what happens. It's in our nature. However, loving the kitchen you have instead of the one you don't is what this cookbook is all about. Small-space living means being intentional about what we bring into our home. That intention applies especially to the kitchen, the epicenter of nourishment for our bodies—and, some might say, our spirits. There is something inherently joyful and fulfilling about bringing healthy, home-cooked food to the table, whether we serve only ourselves or our larger family.

The recipes here are selected for their ease of preparation, the number of ingredients, the space they might require, and how many pans they might use. They are generally designed to feed two people but can be easily scaled up (see page 29). Most of the tools are handheld, as one whisk and a wooden spoon take up much less space than a stand mixer or even a hand mixer. It truly doesn't take much in the way of equipment or tools to create night after night of really good food. Focus and desire alone get you more than halfway there. The rest is cooking your way through these recipes—none of which are complicated, take more than an hour to make, or require more than one or two pans. Additionally, many of these recipes are intended as full, balanced meals in and of themselves. The idea here is to be intentional and intelligent about the use of pans, space, ingredients, and time so that cooking in a small space can be both enjoyable and satisfying.

MY KITCHENS

My primary kitchen is actually a galley located on my family's Maine windjammer, a schooner called the *J. & E. Riggin*. We entertain groups of 24 guests all summer long on multiday adventures, and it is my job to provide scrumptious, beautiful meals three or four times a day, no matter the weather. My counter space, the one on which I work every day, is 2 feet by 3 feet. That's it. The only way a good meal ever emerges from my galley is if I'm on it with the efficiency, organization, planning, and ergonomic work practices.

My other kitchen is in our small house on shore, where I spend the second half of the year writing, creating, and testing recipes with family and friends. The space isn't any bigger than my galley, it's just different.

No matter what kitchen I find myself in, small doesn't mean less beautiful or less flavorful food. And small doesn't mean harder or more time consuming. Actually, a small work space can be smart—and the smarter the work space, the easier the cooking.

MY JOURNEY
(AND YOURS)

I began cooking in very small kitchens on the day after I graduated from college. It was my first job as a mess cook on a sailboat. Up to that point, I'd only worked in restaurant kitchens, which would later seem behemoth in size, with walk-ins galore and miles of countertops. But, like the current trend in tiny houses, I went tiny kitchen when I entered the world of sailing.

Now, having spent most of my professional life cooking on boats (with some educational forays on shore), I've found that the space in which a cook prepares meals to nourish people is actually a little like home decor. The look and feel of your space matters, but it's what happens inside your home that truly defines your life—a good life led is a good life led, whether it's in a tree house or a mansion. So it is with kitchens—good food is good food, whether prepared in a precision-driven, architecturally exquisite kitchen or a tiny galley floating on the water. In each case, the space defines what you might or might not prepare, but not the quality of the ingredients or the craft of the cook preparing those ingredients.

These days, my cooking space is doubly different from what most people are used to. Not only is it tiny, essentially outside, and often tipping to one side or the other, but my range is a woodstove. I don't have electricity, a microwave, a freezer, a walk-in refrigerator, or much storage space at all. As such, my menu is informed by what my woodstove and small galley space can do well. Everything is made by hand. The bread is kneaded by hand, the pesto is chopped by hand, the whipped cream is whisked by hand. (Really, who needs the gym when you have all that?)

However, the fact that I cook on a woodstove and without electricity for half the year isn't especially relevant except to illustrate that no matter the details and eccentricities of a kitchen, the keys to success remain constant: organization, planning, quality ingredients, and creativity. Every space is going to have its challenges; it's up to the cook to figure out how to turn those into opportunities. The fact of the matter is, whether you prefer the adventure of a swift sail on a summer day, the freedom of the road, the exhilarating energy of a small apartment in the city, or the quiet calm of a backyard patio, the basics of cooking are the same no matter what stove you stand beside.

Happy cooking and eating to you!

ANNIE MAHLE
March 2020
44° 5' 47.93" N, 69° 7' 1.47" W
Rockland, Maine

For many summers, I was at home cooking on a woodstove in the small galley kitchen of the Maine windjammer the *J. & E. Riggin* (shown below).

PART 1

setup and strategies

CHAPTER 1

TOOLS AND WORK SPACE

Organization doesn't come naturally to me.
However, the love of efficiency does. Smart spaces,
smart work flow, smart processes—these things
all get me jazzed. And whether your heart glows at the
thought of organizing a space or you just want to
make good food in your little kitchen, it doesn't really
matter. Either way, you've got to be organized.
That means being organized about how things get done
(we'll cover work flow and processes in Chapter 2),
but also about what gets stored where. This chapter is
about the *what* and the *where*.

■

ORGANIZING YOUR WORK AREA

There are all sorts of ways to add storage in a small space. You'll come up with your own ideas that work for you and your personal work flow, but here are a few ideas to get you started.

CONSIDER THE WORK TRIANGLE: stove, fridge, sink. These are the three most common destinations in a kitchen, and we walk between them over and over again. Therefore, they should all be as close together as logistically possible. Try not to have one of these prominent stations standing off alone somewhere. It's awkward and time consuming, for example, to be constantly traveling around the corner to get to the fridge.

ORGANIZE THE SPACE so that the ingredients and tools you use most frequently are close at hand when you need them. The salt and pepper, for example, should be somewhere within reach of the stove. The same is true of the oils you might drizzle in a pan. Now, it's true that in a tiny kitchen, everything is relatively close, but even so, think smartly about the ingredients or equipment you reach for most often and keep them closest.

NOW CONSIDER THE PANTRY. It generally holds items that you are going to get out once and then perhaps put back. Therefore, the pantry can be outside the primary triangle, although if you have the option, including it within that walk flow is wonderful.

SPACE-SAVING TIPS AND TRICKS

When it comes to spare space, any wall, whether inside a cabinet, under a cabinet, or on a cabinet door, is fair game. Even the ceiling is fair game. Any settees, cushioned seating, and the like can give you more storage, too. Look around your small space. Is there extra space above the fridge? Could you put a basket under a table (or a chair)? Could that bare wall receive all the pots and pans? Each kitchen is different, but they all have nooks and crannies that aren't being used. Here are some suggestions for how to fit in all the essential odds and ends.

LIDS. Hanging lids, either on their own or by sliding the pot handle through the opening of the lid handle, gets them out of precious drawer space. Or they can be stored vertically in a rack or a spare space between cupboards.

from top to bottom

Storage in a tiny kitchen requires a thorough accounting of space, from floor to ceiling. Think creatively about *your* space in particular. What little corners of unused space could become storage spots? What blank wall space or cabinet space could be used more smartly?

GO HIGH. The tops of cabinets, the refrigerator, and stand-alone pantry cupboards are all perfect places to store things, whether out on display or tucked away in baskets, boxes, or little shelving units.

GO LOW. Storing big pans or other lesser-used items under the stove, under a shelving unit, and even under the floor (if there's access) are common ways to get a few more items stowed.

GO VERTICAL. Hang everything you can. Pots and pans can be hung over the stove, on the wall, or on the side of an island.

NEST EVERYTHING. When purchasing any dishware, mixing bowls, or pots and pans, choose those that can be stacked together when they're not in use.

MUGS. Mugs gently swaying overhead is a common sight in a boat galley. Think about hanging them under a cabinet, inside a cabinet, or over the sink.

PLATES AND BOWLS. Everything should nest with a very low profile. Choose dishware that tends toward thin lines, stacks cleanly, and takes up little real estate. Also, consider choosing large bowls that can double as plates (or take the place of a plate and superfluous salad bowl). Chapter 5 is dedicated to meals that can be served in a single bowl, rather than on plates or in multiple dishes, and that's where these large dinner bowls could come in handy.

SHEET PANS, TRAYS, PLATTERS, AND CUTTING BOARDS. Store these items vertically in a cabinet, over the fridge, or in that weird space between the fridge and the counter or the stove. If a cutting board has a hole in its corner, it can be hung from a hook or a clever bit of hardware, such as a wooden peg, a square nail, or a copper pipe elbow—whatever complements the decor of your space.

KNIVES. Knives can be stored in a drawer, but a magnetic strip can easily hold them alongside a cabinet or on the backsplash, leaving the drawer for other utensils. A knife block may take up more counter space than is necessary, and it holds more knives than are really needed in most kitchens. If you only have a chef's knife and a paring knife, then even a magnetic strip might be overkill.

POTS AND PANS. They should either nest well or be hung. Sometimes you can also store skillets on their side. Some companies sell pans with removable handles for easier storage, but they tend to be of lesser quality. It is possible, however, to simply forgo most long-handled pans altogether and cook primarily with stockpots and Dutch ovens.

TOOLS. If drawer space is at a minimum, hang your tools or stand them in a tall crock.

Hanging mugs (top), well-nested pans (middle), and a peg for hanging a cutting board (bottom) are all valuable space savers in a small kitchen.

working without "mono-tools"

In this book, mono-tools (tools that do just one thing) such as blenders, stand mixers, slow cookers, and microwaves are considered luxuries, not essentials. The mixing bowls must nest, the bowls and plates must serve more than one purpose, and the appliances must have more than one function.

If you have a mono-tool in a small kitchen, it had better be something fabulous that you feel you can't live without. Rice cookers, microwaves, toasters . . . these appliances all create results that can be achieved in other ways with a tool that takes up less space. Think before you buy: Where will this item be stored? Do you already have another tool that does basically the same thing? How often will you use this item?

One much-loved mono-tool is the slow cooker, which takes up a huge amount of precious real estate and can be easily replaced with a stockpot. Yes, it's true, you can't just turn on a stockpot and leave for work, but there are going to be a few things that just won't work well in a small space. In addition, newer equipment such as multifunction pressure cookers (like the Instant Pot), air fryers, and the like all have their places and their fans, but I'm a pretty low-tech girl. While the recipes in this cookbook can certainly be adapted for these appliances, I've not gone out of my way to make them fit the latest craze. The minimalist kitchen doesn't need much to do a lot.

SPICES. All those little jars of spices and herbs can sometimes take up more space than is necessary. You could instead buy them "in bulk," purchasing only what you need—2 tablespoons, let's say, rather than the full ¼ to ⅓ cup that comes in jars. Store the spices in little baggies in a basket hanging close to the stove or on a pantry shelf. You could also put your most-used spices in jars with magnetic lids and store them on the side of the fridge or on a magnetic strip under cabinets, or you could set up a little spice rack on the inside of a cupboard. Definitely get them off the countertop. I've also seen spices stored in drawers, but in my kitchens, drawer space is always at a premium.

SHELVES. If the items to be stored aren't very tall, adding an extra shelf creates twice the space. Try stacking additional shelves on top of or under already-existing shelves. If a whole shelf takes up too much space, perhaps a corner shelf would work.

WINDOWS. Put one or two shelves across a kitchen window, or install a curtain rod from which you can hang things.

TABLE AND CHAIRS. If space is really tight, a fold-down (or folding) table and chairs is a wonderful way to have seating when you need it—and out of the way when you don't. Sometimes just downsizing a kitchen table and chairs does the trick, or using a half-moon table that fits against a wall. And don't forget to look at the space underneath any seating. If you have a settee, can you store baskets under it? Can you convert the seat to a lid that conceals storage below? If you have chairs with rungs, can you rest baskets on the rungs?

SAME-SIZE CONTAINERS. When items are stored in containers that are all the same size, they are easier to stack and organize and therefore take up less real estate.

RECIPE OR COOKBOOK HOLDER. To get a recipe or cookbook off the counter and out of the way, use a magnetic strip and hardy magnet, a clothespin, or a book holder. If you use a digital device to display your recipes, consider a suction mount that will attach to a wall, fridge, or cabinet door.

THE TOE KICK. This is that 2- to 3-inch span between the base of the cabinet door and the floor. It's usually inaccessible dead space. In a tiny kitchen, using this space for shallow drawers or slides can give a big boost to the storage territory.

BEST EQUIPMENT FOR SMALL SPACES

Different small kitchens are, of course, going to have different essential equipment. RVers and boaters might not want to use anything that plugs in and uses electricity. Apartment dwellers might not have the space to set up a grill. Other cooks might have a grill but not an indoor oven. No matter. For the purposes of this cookbook, I'm going to make a couple of assumptions. I'm assuming you have running water, some kind of refrigeration—even if it's a dorm fridge—and some kind of burner or heat source. I'm not assuming that everyone has a full-size oven, but I do assume that you have at least a toaster oven. If your cooking circumstances are even more rustic—cabin life, off-grid, van life, or any other bucolic and eminently Instagrammable situation—these recipes are totally adaptable to those circumstances.

It will be up to you to decide how important a specific appliance is to how you cook, and how much space you have to dedicate to your appliances and tools. The point is to choose intentionally and know that there may be some things you can't do in your small space. No problem—love the space you have, not the one you don't.

Good food can be created with very little—every pan and tool used for this cookbook can fit into a milk crate. Pinky promise.

I'm a firm believer that a knife, a cutting board, and a pot are all that's needed to make some really awesome food. However, with just a few more items, life can get really creative. What follows are my essentials.

HANDS. Our hands are built to be tools—fingers pressed together to scoop out the last little bits in a bowl, palms pushing firmly to knead bread, whole hands cupped to gently mold meatballs. . . . Our hands are always with us and ready to do the work we ask of them.

CUTTING BOARD. Of course, there's the usual use of the superfunctional cutting board, but it can also substitute as a platter or be placed over the kitchen sink or on the stovetop (make sure the burners are off) to create more counter space.

KNIVES. While a full set looks enticing, all anyone really needs is an 8- or 10-inch chef's knife, a paring knife, and perhaps a serrated bread knife.

TWO CAST-IRON SKILLETS, SMALL AND LARGE, WITH LIDS. Because they are oven-safe, cast-iron skillets are much more versatile than, say, a nonstick skillet with a plastic handle. They can be used as a baking pan and for roasting. The lids are critical for both trapping heat and controlling splatter with anything pan-seared. In a pinch, another skillet or a baking sheet can stand in for a lid.

SAUCEPAN. If you have space for two different-size pans, then a 1.5-quart and a 3-quart would be wonderful, but if not, then a 3-quart pan is probably the most useful and can double as a stockpot if needed.

STOCKPOT OR DUTCH OVEN. This covers all things soup and stew, plus it doubles as a mixing bowl. If you don't have the space, forgo it, and know that the 3-quart saucepan will do if you're cooking for only two people.

ONE OR TWO SHEET PANS. But only if your kitchen has an oven. If not, skip these. If you have a toaster oven, use sheet pans that fit.

WOODEN SPOON, SPATULA, AND TONGS. One of each will do.

POTATO MASHER. Obviously the best tool for making mashed potatoes by hand, a potato masher is also the best tool I've found to mix all of my baking ingredients in one bowl without getting lumps. In addition to potatoes, a masher mushes avocados, bananas, and other soft foods and can smash soft nuts like pecans or walnuts. And if you need a tenderizer, while it's not the full-on hammer, a masher does the trick in a pinch.

WHISK. Own a whisk for whipping cream, making aioli, and mixing vinaigrettes.

BOX GRATER. It's not just for cheese but also for zesting citrus, grating butter for pastries, and shredding carrots or zucchini. You might instead choose a microplane and/or a flat grater if they make more sense for your space.

GLASSES AND MUGS. Consider drinkware that can do double duty—for example, mugs that can be used not only for that crucial cup of coffee in the morning but also for hot soup or a scoop of ice cream, and glasses that can be used not only for drinks but also for serving parfaits and puddings.

INSTANT-READ THERMOMETER. This is the easiest way to tell when meats are ready to be pulled off the heat.

VEGETABLE PEELER. In addition to peeling potatoes, carrots, and such, a peeler can be used to slice cheese and make strips of parsnips, sweet potatoes, zucchini, and other vegetables.

STRAINER AND/OR COLANDER. A strainer will usually take up a little less space than a colander and may be all you need. It also serves as a sifter for flour, cocoa powder, confectioners' sugar, and other powdered pantry staples.

If There's Space . . .

In addition to the essential items above, here is a handful of useful things that are very much worth having if space allows.

MANDOLIN. Several of the recipes in this book call for thinly sliced vegetables and fruit. While a good bit of this work can be done with clever knife work or creative vegetable peeling, a mandolin is a nice tool to have.

HANDHELD (OR IMMERSION) BLENDER. Having beaten and whisked almost everything by hand for years, this is one of only a few electric tools I would choose for my tiny kitchen. It takes the place of a food processor, blender, and mixer all at once. It's the ultimate multitasker, the polar opposite to a mono-tool.

Mugs can do double or triple duty as serving vessels for beverages, desserts, and soups.

no oven?
no problem

With the exception of baked goods, most recipes in this book that call for an oven can also be made in a skillet. When using a skillet in place of an oven, nothing compares to cast iron. The kind of heat that the skillet sustains with this cooking method is a bit rugged for a normal stainless-steel skillet, but a cast-iron skillet will take all sorts of abuse without blinking. Keep in mind, however, that because cast iron has such mass, it takes longer to heat up and also takes longer to cool down. This can affect cooking times.

A lid for your skillet is critical for trapping the heat. It does create a moister heat than an oven will, so those delicious crispy bits and melty edges that come from roasting in an oven aren't going to happen as readily, but it is still possible to achieve a browning effect. You can always leave the lid cracked open to allow some of the moisture to escape, a good technique for those times when you want less steam and more dry heat.

MINI FOOD PROCESSOR. Most food processors are too big for recipes that serve just two people, but these little numbers take up very little space for the workhorses that they are.

BLENDER. Many blenders come with (or you can purchase separately) a small food processor attachment. These duos are nice and can replace the above two items. That said, none of these plug-in appliances are required. They are bonus equipment that make things a little faster and a little more versatile.

TOASTER OVEN. If your kitchen has an oven, then maybe you don't need a toaster oven. On the other hand, if you don't have space for a full oven, then a toaster oven is going to be a very good friend to you. Despite the name, a toaster oven can do way more than just toast. Think of it as a countertop oven that can bake potatoes, broil open-faced sandwiches, roast a Cornish game hen, and, in a pinch, even manage a small batch of cookies while using far less energy than a full-size oven. When you're cooking for just one or two people, it's the versatile champion of a small kitchen.

GET CREATIVE

Small kitchens require a little more ingenuity from the chef to get the job done. While biscuit or doughnut cutters may not have a spot in the kitchen, most of us will have an empty can we can use as a cutter. While not all of us will have space for a rolling pin (or use one that often), when the urge to make a pie strikes, a wine bottle or perhaps a water bottle really does do the trick. Most larger kitchens have a toaster, which does only one thing in our lives—and a lovely thing it is, because who does not love toast? However, toast made in a skillet or in the oven (see page 67) is just as delicious, especially once butter or avocado gets in the game.

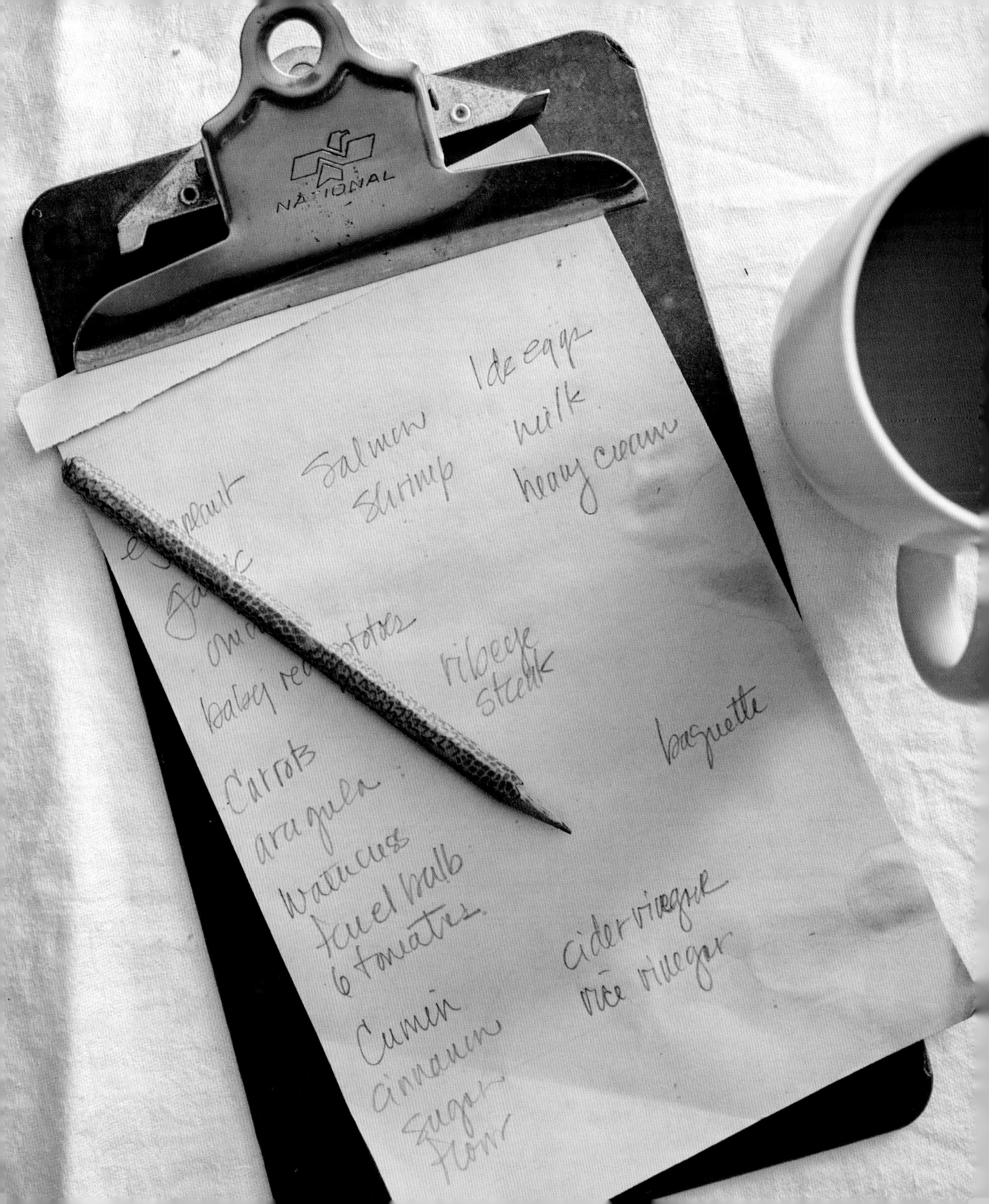

1 dz eggs
milk
heavy cream

Salmon
Shrimp

coconut
Garlic
onions
baby red potatoes

ribeye
steak

baquette

Carrots
arugula
watercress
fennel bulb
6 tomatoes

cider vinegar
rice vinegar

Cumin
cinnamon
sugar
flour

CHAPTER 2

MEAL PLANNING

Understanding the process of planning
a meal is part of any good cook's skill set,
but nowhere is this more critical
than in a tiny kitchen, where missteps can be
amplified by fewer substitution choices
and a moderate array of tools at one's disposal.
Success starts long before the prep work and
carries straight through to cleanup and trash removal.
The more a cook can incorporate good,
smart habits into the
rhythm of the kitchen, the better.

SHOPPING TIPS

When you're grocery shopping for a small kitchen, saying that you shouldn't overpurchase seems like an obvious suggestion. But how do you actually accomplish this feat and still arrive home with enough ingredients for at least a few days' worth of meals?

Plan, Plan, Plan

I'm not an organized person by nature, but I've witnessed it in other people. You know the type—those who just love organizing for the sake of organizing. Having things lined up and in their proper place makes their hearts sing. Yeah, that's not me. *However*, I am organized because I don't like waste—of time or food. I love efficiency in all its forms. And in a small kitchen, being organized is critical to both reducing waste and boosting efficiency. Those of us with small kitchens don't have the luxury of just going to the store and getting a bunch of food without some semblance of a plan. If we did that, we'd run out of room in our tiny fridge and pantry space, and whatever didn't fit would end up sitting out on our tiny counter, cluttering up our precious work space. So, it's important to decide on a menu plan for the week or at least the next several days before shopping.

Shop the Pantry and Fridge First

Before even beginning to write a menu for the week or the next couple of days, pause. Check the pantry and the fridge to find out what you have on hand and what is most perishable and needs to be incorporated into a meal before it dies. Make it a habit to use up what you have before bringing more items into your small kitchen. We all know this advice, but when we arrive at the grocery store without a plan, it's easy to get tempted by all the newest and shiniest things there.

Wait to Shop

In our house, it's become a bit of a game to see how long we can go without making a trip to the grocery store. When someone insists that "there's nothing to eat in this house," I am usually able to get two more dinners out of what's on hand before the next round of shopping. This clearly saves on waste, but also, if you don't have a supersized refrigerator, clearing out the fridge and pantry space before shopping is equally important.

Stay on Top of Your Inventory

When you use up the last of something, put it on the grocery list immediately. As you're creating your menu plan, whether for the week or for a party, be sure to run through the ingredients for all of the recipes to see what you need before heading to the store.

Buy Small

Buy the smallest amount of ingredients that will get the meals made. The fewer things you have left over, the better, even when it comes to dry goods. While you don't want to be stuck without a specific ingredient that you need, you also don't have space for that 20-pound bag of basmati rice on sale at Costco.

Buy in Bulk

While it's obvious that a Sam's Club membership and a case of paper towels are not in a small kitchen's future, there can be advantages to buying "in bulk." When an item is available in a self-serve bulk bin, you can actually purchase *less* than what you'd have to buy if you bought that item prepackaged. This is especially helpful with spices, where all flavor goes to die when they sit on the shelf for a year. Buying fewer and less spices and herbs will keep your tiny stash

fresh and full of flavor and take up much less space than a fully stocked spice rack with the usual-sized bottles. The same is also true for dry goods. Depending on how many people you are typically serving, buying smaller quantities more frequently will help with space saving.

Shop the List

Going to the store with a list and a plan reduces overspending, overshopping, and stress about storage space once the abundance arrives home. Even if you shop at farmers' markets and buy local, you can still plan ahead and know that you'll need, for example, greens for one dish, onions for another, and squash for a third. Then, when you get to the farmers' market, you'll have the flexibility to choose which variety looks most delicious.

Shop with a Full Belly

Try not to shop hungry, since there's no telling what will make it into your shopping cart at such a time. Hunger gets the best of us, and before we know it, we've blown our shopping budget and arrived home with several bags of perishable items only to find we have no room to store them all.

Buy Less and Shop More Often

Making a weekly menu plan and shopping only once a week might not work if you have a small space. If you have a dorm fridge, you might be able to plan only three or four days ahead. No problem. The same rules apply—shop the pantry and the fridge first, make a plan, shop the plan, cook the plan. You'll simply buy less at a time and shop more often.

Cook the Plan

Once you've gone to all the trouble of planning and shopping to a list, then do yourself a favor and actually make the meals you planned. If you just aren't feeling it one night, or find that you've run out of time or energy for that particular dish, see about finding something else that uses up the same ingredients you purchased. We've all had the experience of getting the ingredients home and then finding that the meal we've planned just doesn't sound appealing anymore. No worries. There's no need to be super dogmatic; just get creative. But no fair going to the grocery store again, buying the newer, shinier veggies, and shoving the castoffs to the back of the fridge. Use up what you have!

MAKING THE MOST OF YOUR COUNTER SPACE

Organizing helps greatly with any amount of counter space. The idea is to get anything and everything off your countertop so that it can actually be used to prepare a meal. Especially in a small kitchen, it's critical to get coffeemakers, toasters, and the like off your work space. That's step one. Here are some other ways to optimize your use of that essential surface.

Clean as You Go

With a limited number of dishes and even less space, cleaning as you go is essential. Use any pause in the cooking process to keep up with the dishes. This saves on the number of dishes you need in your kitchen and saves on space as well. If you have the luxury of a two-bay sink, use one side for the drying rack to save on counter space.

Use the Cutting Board Wisely

This is one of my favorite ways to create space in a tiny kitchen: place the cutting board over the sink, on top of the stove, or on top of a rolling shelf unit. Of course, you would only use the stovetop as a cutting-board countertop if you didn't need the burners. If you clean as you go, the sink should usually be available. Just move the cutting board when you need access to the sink, and then return the cutting board when you're done.

Go Vertical (Again)

As with many storage solutions, going vertical with your prep can buy you lots of space. As you're preparing ingredients for a meal—measuring, chopping, peeling, mixing, and so on—stash them in bowls and stack them. Stack the bowls in the order of use, if you want to get really tidy. I sometimes also use a sheet pan or cutting board as a layer in my stack of prepped ingredients. If you've got enough space for a big cutting board that can accommodate a lot of prep work, or if you like to prep and cook as you go, it's possible that using bowls to stack ingredients might not even be necessary.

Use the Unusual

When counter space is at a premium, smart cooks get creative. Use the dining table, a chair, a stool, shelves, the top of the fridge, or a basket to keep items off your precious work space while you finish up your meal. If you have the space for it, a small or movable island works super well in a tiny kitchen. I've heard of people using the bathtub to hold dirty dishes and coming back to them later once the guests are gone. (I've only done that for dirty laundry that needs to be stashed to make room for company, but hey, it's a creative idea.) Like I said, smart cooks get creative!

Think It Through

Run through the recipes and processes in your mind ahead of time so that you've made sure you've got space for all of the steps. You don't want to be standing in the kitchen with a hot pan that just came out of the oven and no place to put it.

mise, mise, mise

Mise en place is the French phrase for "everything in its place," and it is well used in the restaurant world. Prepping ahead and being prepared is important in every kitchen, whether it's a big restaurant kitchen or a little postage stamp of a kitchen. The more prepared we are, the smoother the whole process goes—and it's much better than rushing to chop onions when the oil is already in the pan and smoking away.

KITCHEN CHOREOGRAPHY

In restaurant kitchens, where chefs and their sous chefs are constantly moving around with sharp knives, hot pans, and heavy pots full of boiling things, they keep from bumping into each other by calling out verbal cues. It's a shorthand of sorts, and I teach it to all of my assistants and apprentices in the galley to be sure everyone stays safe. You simply call out where you are and the items to watch for. "Behind," "knife in the sink," "sharps coming over," "hot coming over," and "hot pan in the sink" are all common shout-outs.

Because it's so busy and everyone is focused on their job, the safety shout might not register until it's too late. So we use a call-and-response system in the galley, just like we do on deck. When the captain, my husband, calls, "Ready about," the crew responds with a "ready about" as a way of confirming that they have heard and understood the order. Same in the galley. When I call, "Hot pan in the sink," my galley gang calls it back to me, and if they don't, I repeat it to make sure that the warning registers in their conscious mind, not just in the way-back recesses.

Back in my kitchen at home, we use the same verbal warnings because, invariably, my husband wants to be standing exactly where I'm moving, and vice versa. This shorthand helps us move around our tiny space like we're dancing in harmony.

Calling out to helpers in a tiny kitchen space helps avoid collisions.

CROWD CONTROL

While small kitchens are definitely best suited for serving only a few people, sharing a meal with a larger group of friends and family can be wonderful. And no problem. Don't think twice about having friends over for a beer and burgers or hosting a Sunday family dinner. Cooking for a gathering in a small kitchen just requires much of what we've already touched on—planning and organization.

Scaling Up

The recipes in this book are designed to make just two servings in order to reduce the amount of leftovers, which are tough to store in small spaces. The idea is not that you will always only be serving two people, but that you can scale up the recipes as needed to serve more people without ending up with a lot of leftover food.

There are, however, a couple of adjustments that might need to be made depending on the specific recipe. For example, when you're cooking a greater volume of food, the cooking time may increase slightly, so pay attention to what the final temperature should be or what the dish should look like when it's fully cooked.

Also, with larger batches, you may need to slightly reduce the total amount of liquid in a dish. For example, let's say you're tripling a recipe that will be eventually be simmered to evaporate some of the liquid. If you triple the volume of liquid, you'll have to simmer the dish for a much longer time to evaporate the necessary volume of liquid, which could potentially lead to a mushy dish. In a case like this, I recommend reducing the total (tripled) volume of liquid by one-fourth or one-third. You can always add more liquid if you need it.

Strategies for Entertaining

The more planning and cooking you can get done before guests arrive, the better life will be, so choose recipes that can sit for a while as your guests arrive, get settled, and have an appetizer. Typically, I try to have almost all the food ready except for maybe one or two last-minute tasks. Once everyone is focused on drinks and conversation, I'll slip away, finish the last few things, and then call everyone to the table. It helps to have guests occupied elsewhere for a second so that I can concentrate on the final touches without getting distracted (although friends are always a lovely distraction).

As with many strategies for small spaces, those for feeding a crowd are applicable to kitchens and homes of all sizes. It's just that everything counts for more when you are working and living in a small space. Here are a few additional tips:

BE REALISTIC. Know how many people will actually fit well in your space. If you can serve a maximum of six, don't try to cram in more people. Also, how many extra plates, bowls, sets of cutlery, and glasses does your dining space allow? Our kitchen table can fit

a maximum of eight people who really love each other before we have to surrender and take over another room with a larger table or get everyone outside. In the colder months, we just have more frequent dinners with fewer guests.

CLEAR THE SPACE. Move any unwanted furniture or items out of the rooms where your guests will be.

GET OUTSIDE. If it's possible and the weather allows, outdoor entertaining solves many of the challenges of small kitchens. While these recipes don't assume that a grill is part of your kitchen equipment, if you've got one, use it! Many of these recipes can be easily adapted to direct grilling or using a pan or skillet on the grill.

CLEAN UP SMART

Just as with everything else in a small kitchen, dealing with waste and trash takes a little more thought and preparation. Cleanliness and sanitation are important aspects of any kitchen management, but never more so than in a small kitchen, where buildup of waste will be much more immediately apparent and offensive. The final cleanup stages of any meal are just as important as the fun beginnings when it comes to healthy—and

good-smelling—small-space living. Do yourself a favor and just deal with waste quickly and efficiently.

Recycling

Having separate bins for plastic, paper, metal, and glass may not be possible (or necessary, if you have single-stream recycling services), but having one recycling bag or bin somewhere convenient might work. Also, while bigger spaces can absorb the lingering smells of days-old cans and jars, in a small kitchen those smells might waft right under your nose more often than not. Making a regular habit of removing these items from your living space is critical, whether that means having a larger recycling bin outdoors, going to the dump once a week, and/or having a sturdy lid to contain the offenders until they can be carted off.

Trash

A small trash can takes up less floor space than a big one, obviously. Some kitchens might be so small that having a trash can at all is a decadent use of space, and a small bag hanging on a cabinet knob will have to do.

Perhaps more importantly, a small trash can helps prevent offending odors. The faster the bin fills up, the more often the trash needs to be taken out and the shorter the time that the garbage sits around inside the house.

Composting

Every space will have an optimal way of dealing with kitchen scraps without attracting bugs or four-legged creatures. The system we use on our schooner, the *Riggin*, took several years to perfect, but it works well. We store all of our food scraps in 5-gallon buckets with tight-fitting lids—the kind you can get at the hardware store. We cart them off the boat at the end of a trip and schlep them to the compost pile in our backyard. The pile gets layered with any shredded office paper and cardboard that has accumulated over the same period of time. In a different type of small kitchen, it might be that instead of a 5-gallon bucket, it's a 1-gallon bucket that gets emptied every other day or so.

Of course, there are lots of resources on worm, barrel, basement, and backyard composting. Find the system that works for your space. It may take some trial and error, but the reduction in trash is worth the effort. City dwellers will have very different solutions for dealing with waste from those who live in the country, on the water, or on the road. Having a plan is what matters. It goes without saying that disposing of trash safely and responsibly must be a part of any good plan for dealing with household waste.

A small silicone compost box can hook onto a cabinet door while you are cooking so it doesn't take any counter space.

dealing with smells

No matter how quickly you take out the trash, the ghost of last night's meal will always make its way into the following morning. It's just part of living in a small space—everything smells at least a little bit like what you cooked the night before. To mitigate this downside of small space living, try the following:

- Always use a fan if you have one.

- Open the windows if the weather allows.

- Use a lid to at least halfway cover anything in a skillet.

- Clean up well when the meal is done.

- Do all of the dishes, wipe the stovetop, clean the countertop, empty the sink drain, and take out the garbage if you can.

CHAPTER 3

CREATIVE KITCHEN

Many of the recipes in this book
are designed to be an entire meal
unto themselves. However, taking a bit of one
and combining it with other ingredients
can expand your repertoire to include
entirely new and different meals. It's also
a great way to use up leftovers.
This chapter details numerous suggestions
for how to creatively make use of every
last bit of food from a prior meal—a good skill
for the space-conscious and
budget-conscious alike.

TRANSFORM YOUR LEFTOVERS

Guests and friends often ask what I like to cook most. What I love isn't a specific recipe to cook, but rather a way of cooking. I love to make dinner from nothing. And by "nothing," I mean the sort of nothing embodied in the statement "There's *nothing* to eat in this house/refrigerator/cupboard." It's the sort of "nothing" that has my girls opening up the fridge and standing there cooling off the kitchen while they gaze unfocused into shelves full of mysterious and somehow unapproachable containers of leftovers. There's some of this, a little of that, and not much of anything. The little bits of who-knows-what get arranged and rearranged in the refrigerator, but no one is brave enough to figure out how to use them.

I come from a family dedicated to using leftovers. My dad took leftovers seriously; he took them to work for lunch during the week, and on the weekends, he and my brothers would wipe out any prepared food left in the refrigerator. As the only girl in the family, I had to elbow my way in if I wanted anything other than the absolute dregs. However, while my family honed its hockey-checking skills competing for the leftovers, others complain that leftovers are boring, whining, "Who wants to have that again anyway?"

Eating leftovers is not always about having the same meal again.

I think of them as the building blocks, or a starting point, for an entirely different meal. Leftovers are actually a great way to boost flavor in subsequent meals because they already have flavor built into them.

In the same way that soup or chili is even better on the second day, leftovers can be, too. This makes them perfect catalysts for weeknight meals of soup, frittata, pasta, quesadillas, pizza, or omelets. These delicious leftover-inspired meals are also among the hardest to replicate in an actual recipe because we rarely have the same set of leftovers on any given day. Therefore, what follows is really more of a guide—a tool to help you adjust according to what you have on hand.

Soup

Nothing beats a steaming bowl of mouthwatering soup for comfort food. Just think how often we turn to chicken noodle soup when we are feeling out of sorts. Considering how easy it is to make soup with whatever you already have on hand, it rises through the ranks as the perfect food, both for snowy days and for those days when it's too hot to turn on a burner (think chilled soups!).

The beauty of soup is that it can be made from little bits of leftover this and that—things that might not add up to a meal on their own. And while following a recipe is a good fallback when you just can't think about one more thing, there is almost nothing that can't be made into a warm, flavorful soup with the simple addition of well-sautéed onions and garlic and some chicken or vegetable broth. If you are not vegetarian, bacon or pancetta is a sure bet as well. Here are some basic steps for making soup from leftovers. The results will be both frugal and flavorful.

1. **Consider the broth.** It's easy to make simple, flavorful broths should you have these sorts of leftovers on hand:

   - Bones from a whole roasted Cornish game hen (see the recipes on pages 197 and 198), chicken, or roast beef can be simmered in water with onions, carrots, and celery for an impromptu broth. It won't be as full-flavored as true stock, but it's leaps above plain water.

   - Hard rinds from cheeses such as Parmigiano-Reggiano can be saved and then simmered in several cups of water to flavor any Italian-themed soup.

   - Vegetable scraps that would normally go into the compost can be covered with water and simmered to make a vegetable broth.

   - And for a flavor-packed broth, combine bones, cheese rinds, and vegetable scraps to make the base for a fabulous soup or pasta dish.

However, making homemade broth is not even a little bit necessary. Store-bought broth will work beautifully and makes for a really quick dinner on the fly.

2. **Choose three things** from your fridge that seem like they will go together: mashed potatoes, roasted chicken, and kale. Pan-fried fish, julienned veggies sautéed in soy, and some miso. Salsa and cilantro, chili-rubbed steak, and roasted portabella mushrooms. Of course, these are just examples, and you won't have these exact combinations, nor am I suggesting that you should. But they would all make excellent soups. Choosing only three main items for your soup will help you focus on what will taste good together and decreases the likelihood that you'll end up with the unsavory-sounding "everything-but-the-kitchen-sink soup" or "leftovers soup." A good rule of thumb is 2 cups of leftovers for every 3 cups of broth.

3. **Sauté onions and garlic** (and bacon, if you please) in butter or olive oil until the onions are very soft and translucent, 7 to 10 minutes. Season well with salt and pepper. Add perhaps a little tomato paste and a splash of red or white wine (red for tomato-based soups and white for creamy soups).

4. **Add your broth** and bring to a simmer. Add the rest of your ingredients and bring to a simmer again. Taste, and add salt or pepper if needed.

5. **Consider the texture.** You can leave the soup rustic and chunky or purée it, if you have a blender or immersion blender.

6. **Garnish with herbs,** coarsely chopped or minced. Fresh herbs add flavor and give a nice pop of color. I usually use basil, chives, parsley, or dill, adding just one or, at the most, two.

7. **Add crusty bread,** good butter, and a salad, and you've got a whole meal from a bunch of little bits.

Omelet

An omelet is a perfect breakfast meal, of course, but it is also very good for dinner—full of protein, quick, and even elegant. Add a warm baguette and a mixed greens salad dressed with good extra-virgin olive oil and fresh lemon juice, and you have an easy, nutritious meal in no time flat.

The point is to use whatever bits of leftovers you have hanging around in the refrigerator. It helps to heat the leftovers in a separate pan first so that you aren't cooking the eggs too long while waiting for the cold ingredients to warm up.

Leftover roast beef? Make a beef and red onion omelet with feta. Leftover roast chicken? Make a chicken, tomato, and scallion omelet. You get the idea.

A good rule of thumb for a hearty one-person omelet is to use 3 eggs, ½ cup of leftovers, and ¼ cup of cheese per omelet. I like my omelets nice and cheesy, but if you prefer a little less, feel free to reduce the amount.

queen of substitutions

Most of the time, my kitchen is out on the water, where a last-minute trip to the grocery store is out of the question. This means that I've gotten good at substituting ingredients and being creative with what's on hand. In this book, I've listed some substitution ideas with the basic recipes so that you, too, can think about your meals creatively.

Pizza

Pizza is a perfect way to use up leftovers that didn't find their way into bellies the first time around. Small bits of cheese, one or two strips of crumbled bacon, roasted vegetables, grilled chicken breast—almost anything is fair game. Indulge in a little creativity while satisfying the part of you that likes to use up everything in the refrigerator.

For one large pizza, about 12 inches in diameter, the ratio for little bits of this and that should be:

- 1 cup tomato sauce (if you like)
- ½ pound grated and/ or crumbled cheese
- ½ pound cooked meat, such as sausage, prosciutto, bacon, or salami
- ½ pound cooked vegetables, such as asparagus, broccoli, broccoli rabe, onions, and/or peppers, or ½ pound uncooked tender vegetables, such as sliced tomatoes or spinach

Homemade dough is wonderful, but if you don't have time to make the dough, you can usually find it in the deli or prepared foods section of your grocery store, refrigerated and ready to roll out.

salty talk

Salt is such an interesting and essential ingredient— too little and a dish has no flavor; too much and it's all we can taste. Most of the recipes in this book call for a "pinch" of kosher salt, which equals a little less than ¼ teaspoon. When you're measuring, the finer the grain, the more salt by weight. Meaning, for example, that ¼ teaspoon of Morton's kosher salt is going to weigh more (and be saltier) than ¼ teaspoon of Diamond kosher salt because Morton's has a finer grain than Diamond.

That doesn't even begin to cover the differences in all the kinds and forms of salt. In recipes for lots of people with lots of ingredients, the vagaries between brands matter less. But in these recipes, which are designed for two people and call for such a small amount of salt, it matters a good deal. I tested all of these recipes with Morton's kosher salt. Many chefs prefer to use Diamond salt, but I can't always get that way up here in the far Northeast. You might find that you can't get Morton's in your area. That's okay. The point here is to use salt sparingly in these recipes until you get the hang of what a pinch of your brand looks, feels, and tastes like. You can always add more salt, but it's tough to adjust a recipe once it has too much.

Pasta

Almost any sort of pasta will work when you're building a dinner from leftovers. Spaghetti, linguini, bucatini, and angel hair are classics. Gemelli, orecchiette, and penne are equally wonderful. Shorter noodles work, too, but not if they are too small; leave the orzo, ditalini, and the like to side dishes or soups. If you're heading in a non-Italian direction, try ramen, soba, and udon.

For your non-noodle components, you might consider the following:

ONION AND GARLIC. Of course, anything in the allium family is a good place to start. Shallots are beautiful and give a more elegant flavor. Leeks or ramps would also be delicious. Just be sure to slice the leeks thinly so that they get fully cooked.

TOMATOES. Commercially canned, home-canned, fresh, large, or cherry—they're all good!

PROTEIN AND VEGETABLES. Can we just say the sky is the limit here? Pick three items from your fridge that work well in combination.

CHEESE AND DAIRY. For garnishing and serving, Parmesan is the obvious choice, but other hard cheeses, like Pecorino or Asiago, are also good. Ricotta, chèvre, feta, and farmer's cheese all make a nice creamy sauce, as do crème fraîche and heavy cream.

SPICES AND HERBS. Pasta is a perfect place for fresh herbs. Basil is a no-brainer, but adding a little fresh thyme, rosemary, or sorrel can make a beautiful dish. Spices such as red pepper flakes and cumin are also lovely. If you are using Asian noodles, then ginger, garlic, lemongrass, and turmeric are all fair game.

Crêpes

Essentially a skinny pancake, these little beauties are made individually in a small skillet rather than on a griddle. They can be either savory or sweet and as elegant or rustic as you like. Follow the instructions for making the crêpes on page 73, and then add your own fillings.

SWEET: Serve with jam or jelly, seared fruits, flavored whipped creams, toasted nuts, or just plain Nutella.

SAVORY: Poached eggs never go amiss when served with crêpes. Add steamed vegetables, a little flaky fish, and a sprinkle of cheese. Crêpes are delicate, so think about delicate ingredients to go with them, like asparagus, crabmeat, and hollandaise sauce rather than seared beef chili and bell peppers, for example, which are better suited to the heartier tortilla.

USE IT UP

Cooking for only two people can be an interesting endeavor because so many ingredients come in amounts that will be more than what you need, leaving you with a lot left over. For example, using cauliflower in any recipe requires purchasing an entire head. It's a rare recipe that uses a whole head of cauliflower for two people—not that it can't be done, but it certainly would take center stage. What to do with the other half a head of cauliflower, or half a can of beans, or handful of diced tomatoes . . . ? Certainly you could find recipes, here and elsewhere, that offer solutions to this quandary, but even better is just to know all the great ways you can use up those left-behind ingredients—folded into other dishes, dressed up as side dishes, transformed into flavorful condiments, and more.

The following list focuses on those ingredients that are used in the recipes in this book, and especially those that are called for as only a portion of the whole amount, leaving behind half a head, a cup's worth from a container, a few spoonfuls from a can, and so on. They also include some specialty ingredients that are called for in the book's recipes,

since you might be looking for other ways to use them. Of course, it's up to you to judge how much space you want to dedicate to special sauces and ingredients, such as pomegranate molasses, harissa paste, and roasted red peppers. They certainly can kick up a recipe into high gear and make your taste buds happy, but you don't want to fall into the trap of using a specialty ingredient only once and then having it simply take up space. The suggestions that follow will help you use those ingredients more frequently.

Banana peppers

Mixed with mayo on an Italian sub with mortadella or soppressata

In salsa with tomatoes and avocado

With lightly salted raw carrots and golden beets, marinated in the banana pepper juice

Beets

Steamed with carrots and then marinated with olives and olive juice

Pickled with onions, black pepper, and whole cloves

Steamed, sliced, and then tossed with a little mayo and grainy mustard and served over greens

Buttermilk

In pancakes

With harissa paste or chipotles en adobo as a dressing

With dill and chives in a chilled soup

In mashed potatoes

Cannellini beans

Mixed with tomatoes, parsley, and garlic and served as a side dish to grilled chicken

Drizzled with extra-virgin olive oil and pomegranate molasses or balsamic vinegar

In soup with pancetta, onions, celery, carrots, and thyme

Puréed with garlic, walnuts, and anchovies to make a spread

Cauliflower

Mixed with kale pesto and capers

Roasted with sage and
brown-butter bread crumbs

Mashed in place of rice

Au gratin with garlic, black
pepper, and Parmesan cheese

Clam stock

As broth for chowder

As broth for fish soup

As a sauce with lemon, cream,
and dill over fish or with pasta

Coconut milk

With chicken and curry paste
over jasmine rice

In soup with garlic, ginger,
lemongrass, and lime

In a pineapple smoothie

With pork and cabbage over
rice noodles

Fennel

Shaved and tossed with
currants, hazelnuts, and mint

Roasted with red bell peppers
and finished with fontina

Thinly sliced with tomatoes
and dill

In a tartlet with chèvre and olives

Figs (dried)

Stewed with ginger and
orange zest

Sautéed in butter with carrots

In granola

With oatmeal

Harissa paste

With Greek yogurt and roasted eggplant

With buttermilk as a dressing

With lemon and olive oil drizzled on couscous

Heavy cream

Whipped and then layered with cake and sugared fruit

In a pasta sauce with caramelized onions and garlic

In a puréed vegetable or potato soup

Lentils

Added to a quick soup

Puréed with tahini for a dip or spread

Combined with cucumbers and parsley in a salad

Combined with arugula, labneh, and dukkah on toast

Peas

In a soup with chicken and orzo

Mashed with lemon and dill

Spread on toast with tomatoes and tahini

Mixed with Greek yogurt, cilantro, and lime

Pomegranate molasses

In a cocktail with grapefruit juice and vodka

With tonic water and lime

In a marinade for steak

Tossed with cherries, mint, and Greek yogurt

Pork (ground)

Cooked in chili with beans, peppers, onions, chili powder, and tomatoes

Cooked with onions, garlic, and ginger and served in a lettuce wrap with peanuts and cilantro

Cooked with tomatoes, onions, bell peppers, basil, and oregano and served over pasta

Pumpkin purée

In soup with heavy cream

In pumpkin mousse

In pancakes

In pumpkin Alfredo pasta with cream and sage

Radicchio

Shaved and tossed with orange juice, olives, and capers

One outer leaf as a serving bowl

Pan-seared with tomatoes and garlic and served over polenta

In a gratin baked with garlic, cream, and cheese

Roasted red pepper

With cannellini beans, roasted radicchio, and preserved lemons

In pasta with hot Italian sausage and kale

Tossed with other roasted veggies

Sambal oelek

Smashed with an avocado and lime on toast or as a dip

Mixed with mayo as a dressing

With ground pork wrapped in romaine lettuce leaves

With sour cream and lime in an Asian-inspired slaw

Sour cream

With chives, broccoli, and baked potato

Swirled into tomato soup

On tacos

In a black bean dip with lime, cilantro, and tomatoes

Tomatoes (canned)

Tossed with stale bread, extra-virgin olive oil, capers, olives, and fresh basil

Sautéed with onions and garlic as a medium for poaching eggs

In a sauce with garlic and cream served over grilled fish and polenta

Sautéed with garlic, onions, peppers, and kale with harissa paste

Turkey (ground)

As a turkey burger mixed with cheddar, cilantro, and salsa

Mixed with sage, garlic, fennel seeds, and salt for turkey sausage patties

Made into meatballs and served in a sub

Yogurt

With berries and honey in a soup

With walnuts and raisins on toast

In a chicken salad with curry and lime

In a spread with extra-virgin olive oil and sea salt, served with pita

recipes for the small kitchen

Toast in a Skillet,
page 67

CHAPTER 4

QUICK AND LIGHT

These recipes are meant to be low impact,
meaning they don't take much time,
don't use all that many ingredients,
and don't dirty many dishes. Some can do
triple duty as a snack, breakfast, or light meal,
depending on your mood
and appetite. All offer lots of flavor
with little fuss.

Snacks and Appetizers

Sometimes all you need to feel a little fancy
is a simple but delicious appetizer
to prime your taste buds
(and those of your guests, if you're entertaining).
Then again, sometimes a delicious snack
is all you need to feel focused,
whole, and ready to face the rest of your day.
These recipes can do both.

PISTACHIO DUKKAH with OLIVE OIL and BAGUETTE

Dukkah is a habit-forming Egyptian condiment composed of crushed spices, seeds, and nuts. Most often it is made with the deeper Middle Eastern spices like the ones used here, but there are many variations on the same beautiful theme. The idea is to tear off a small bit of bread and dunk it in the olive oil and then the dukkah. The olive oil helps the dukkah stick to the bread.

Makes 1 cup

¼ cup sesame seeds

¼ teaspoon ground allspice

¼ teaspoon ground cinnamon

¼ teaspoon ground cumin

¼ teaspoon ground ginger

Pinch of kosher salt

¾ cup shelled and salted pistachios

Extra-virgin olive oil, for serving

Baguette, for dunking

1. Heat a small skillet over medium-high heat and add the sesame seeds, allspice, cinnamon, cumin, ginger, and salt. Cook, stirring constantly, for 1 to 2 minutes, until the spices begin to smoke ever so slightly. Add the pistachios and stir for another minute. Transfer the mixture to a plate to cool.

2. Either finely mince the mixture on a cutting board or grind it coarsely in a small food processor.

3. Serve with the olive oil and baguette.

Switch It Up!
MORE WAYS TO USE DUKKAH
On top of roasted carrots with chèvre | As a coating on seared salmon or tuna | Sprinkled on kale with garlic | Over roasted tomatoes and quinoa with labneh

CHOCOLATE BAGUETTE WITH OLIVE OIL AND SEA SALT

This simple dish adds just a little sweetness to the end of your meal. My daughters used to request it as a snack, and sometimes they got it as a treat. This is the time to use your very best extra-virgin olive oil, chocolate, and sea salt. If you like the crunchy, salty texture of coarse sea salt, then by all means use it. If you would prefer just a hint of salt, use a finer grain. I don't give an amount for the salt because the measurement depends on what type of salt you use and your own palate. Start with a little—you can always add more.

A toaster oven comes in handy here, as some small ovens don't have a broil option. If neither is available to you, toast the baguette in a skillet, remove from the heat, sprinkle with chocolate, cover, and let the chocolate melt under the lid.

Serves 2

4 generous slices of baguette

Very good extra-virgin olive oil

Sea salt

¼ cup shaved high-quality bittersweet chocolate, such as Callebaut or Valrhona

1. Preheat the broiler in your oven.

2. Lay the baguette slices on a baking pan. Drizzle lightly with olive oil and sprinkle sparingly with sea salt. Top the slices with the chocolate, dividing it evenly among them.

3. Set the baking pan on the lower rack in the oven. Broil for about 1 minute, until the chocolate has melted. Watch closely, as the chocolate can easily scorch. Serve immediately for maximum chocolate meltiness.

SPANISH TORTA

While this dish is absolute comfort food and makes a fabulous dinner when served with a salad, I've also been known to serve Spanish torta as an appetizer. Sliced thinly and served with a tomatoey brava sauce (page 59), Manchego cheese, and some good-quality Manzanilla or Campo Real olives, it's a special starter.

Of course, you could stray from the traditional and try myriad combinations. Roasted veggies, pancetta, kalamata olives, and hearty greens are all delicious choices.

Serves 2

- 12 ounces baby Yukon Gold potatoes, thinly sliced (about 20 potatoes)
- 1 medium onion, sliced (about 1 cup)
- ¾ teaspoon kosher salt
- Freshly ground black pepper
- ¼ cup extra-virgin olive oil
- 4 eggs

1. Heat a small cast-iron or nonstick skillet over medium-high heat. Combine the potatoes, onion, salt, several grinds of pepper, and olive oil in a medium bowl and mix well. Transfer to the skillet, reduce the heat to medium-low, and cover. Fry until the potatoes are tender and creamy, about 20 minutes.

2. In the same bowl, beat the eggs with a pinch of salt. When the potatoes are done, drain the oil from the skillet and transfer the potatoes to the bowl of eggs. Stir fairly quickly to distribute the heat of the potatoes, and then return the mixture to the skillet over medium-low heat.

3. When the bottom of the torta is cooked, 3 to 4 minutes, loosen the egg from the edges of the skillet with a spatula. Place a plate on top of the skillet and then flip the skillet over, so that the torta drops onto the plate. Slide the torta back into the skillet and cook the other side for 2 to 3 minutes.

4. Flip the torta onto a round serving platter. Slice into wedges to serve.

BAKED MANCHEGO WITH TOASTED ALMONDS AND WARM SHERRY VINAIGRETTE

Honestly, just add a salad and it's dinner. Or a delicious appetizer. I'm hooked on baked cheese of any sort. Manchego is a tangy, nutty Spanish cheese with traditional basket-weave hash marks on the rind, and it pairs well with the almonds and sherry vinegar. But keep in mind there are lots of ways to do baked cheese: baked Brie with toasted walnuts and lemon marmalade, maybe some baked Gouda with apple slices and Dijon vinaigrette, or whatever tickles your fancy.

Serves 2

BAKED MANCHEGO

6 ounces Manchego cheese, wax edges removed, sliced into ¼-inch wedges

1 teaspoon extra-virgin olive oil

¼ cup panko bread crumbs

TOASTED ALMONDS

1 tablespoon extra-virgin olive oil

3 tablespoons sliced almonds

Tiny pinch of kosher salt

SHERRY VINAIGRETTE

2 tablespoons extra-virgin olive oil

1 tablespoon minced garlic (about 3 cloves)

¼ cup piquillos or roasted red peppers, thinly sliced

2 tablespoons minced fresh flat-leaf parsley

2 teaspoons sherry vinegar

Pinch of kosher salt

Crusty bread, for serving

1. Preheat the oven to 450°F (230°C). Lay a paper towel on a plate.

2. To make the baked Manchego, lightly brush the cheese slices with the oil. Put the bread crumbs on a plate and press the cheese slices into them, coating both sides. Place on an ovenproof platter and bake for 7 to 8 minutes, until the cheese starts to melt.

3. To toast the almonds, heat the oil in a small saucepan over medium-high heat. Add the almonds and cook, stirring frequently, for 1 to 2 minutes, until the almonds have become golden brown. Transfer with a slotted spoon to the towel-lined plate and sprinkle with the salt.

4. To make the vinaigrette, add the oil to the pan you used to toast the almonds and set it over medium heat. Add the garlic and sauté until fragrant, 30 seconds to 1 minute. Add the piquillos, parsley, vinegar, and salt and stir to heat everything thoroughly, then remove from the heat.

5. Spoon the warm vinaigrette over the baked cheese slices and top with the toasted almonds. Serve immediately with crusty bread.

FRIED SEA-SALTED ALMONDS

Bacon is a special treat in our house these days, but when we have it, we save the flavorful fat for other dishes. While for me the idea that bacon fat is a high indulgence is still ingrained, what we are learning about fats is that the good ones come from healthy vegetables or sustainably raised animals. Healthy local pigs give us better bacon fat. Hence, this addictive snack.

Makes ¾ cup

3 tablespoons bacon fat

¾ cup whole almonds

Fat pinch of Maldon sea salt or other flaky salt

1. Lay a paper towel on top of a plate.

2. Heat the fat in a high-sided skillet over medium-high heat for 1 to 2 minutes, until an almond added to the pan sizzles. Carefully add the rest of the almonds. Cook, stirring continuously, for 2 to 4 minutes, until the skin of the first nut cracks a little (you'll hear it). Then transfer the almonds to the towel-lined plate.

3. Sprinkle the salt on the almonds while they are hot. Let cool before serving.

PATATAS BRAVAS

Essentially potatoes with a flavorful tomato sauce, patatas bravas is a dish well loved in Spain and often found on tapas menus. The sauce is even better if made a day ahead. The almonds give it a soft, lightly sweet taste; if you like a spicier sauce, add a dash of Tabasco. Use up any leftover sauce with pasta, with eggs, in soup, or on hot garlicky greens.

Serves 2

POTATOES

4 medium red potatoes, skin on, cut into 6 wedges each

Kosher salt

1 tablespoon extra-virgin olive oil

Freshly ground black pepper

BRAVA SAUCE

3 tablespoons slivered almonds

2 tablespoons extra-virgin olive oil

⅓ cup minced shallot (about 1 shallot)

1 tablespoon minced garlic (about 3 cloves)

½ teaspoon paprika

1 cup diced tomatoes (canned is fine)

1 tablespoon sherry vinegar

Pinch of kosher salt

Pinch of red pepper flakes

1. Preheat the oven to 400°F (200°C).

2. To toast the almonds for the brava sauce, sprinkle them on a roasting pan and toast in the oven until light brown, 5 to 7 minutes. Transfer them to a small bowl and set aside. Return the roasting pan to the oven.

3. To prepare the potatoes, put them in a medium stockpot, add enough water to cover them, and salt it well. Bring to a boil over high heat and boil for 4 minutes. Remove ½ cup of the potato water (for the sauce, in case it needs to be thinned) and set aside. Then drain the potatoes (they will not be fully cooked) and return them to the pot. Toss gently with the oil, a pinch of salt, and a few grinds of pepper and transfer to the hot roasting pan. Bake for 35 to 45 minutes, until they are nicely browned on the outside.

4. Meanwhile, make the sauce: Heat the oil in a small saucepan over medium-high heat. Add the shallot and sauté for 3 minutes. Add the garlic, paprika, and toasted almonds and sauté for 3 minutes, or until the shallots and garlic are soft. Add the tomatoes, vinegar, salt, and red pepper flakes. Turn down the heat and simmer for 30 minutes.

5. When the sauce is done, check the texture. If it seems too thick, add enough of the reserved potato water to thin it. It will be chunky, which lends a rustic flair, but if you prefer a more refined look, purée the sauce in a small food processor.

6. Serve the roasted potatoes with the sauce drizzled on top or in a bowl on the side for dipping.

GARLICKY SHRIMP WITH GARLIC CHIPS

With all of the flavor in this dish, we sometimes just have it with a salad and a bit of bread and call it good. This recipe calls for oil in the marinade as well as oil in which to sauté the shrimp. All that oil makes a great garlicky dipping sauce for an authentic, crusty bread, if you're into that kind of thing—and I definitely am.

Serves 2 to 4

SHRIMP

½ pound medium shrimp, peeled and deveined

1 tablespoon minced garlic (about 3 cloves)

2 tablespoons extra-virgin olive oil

2 teaspoons grated lemon zest (from about 1 lemon)

1 tablespoon fresh lemon juice

½ teaspoon paprika

Pinch of kosher salt

2 tablespoons minced fresh flat-leaf parsley

GARLIC CHIPS

2 tablespoons extra-virgin olive oil

⅓ cup thinly sliced garlic (6 to 8 cloves)

Pinch of kosher salt

1. To make the shrimp, combine the shrimp, 2 teaspoons of the garlic, and the oil, lemon zest, lemon juice, paprika, and salt in a large bowl and mix gently. Set the mixture aside to marinate for at least 30 minutes.

2. To make the garlic chips, lay a paper towel on a plate. Heat the oil in a medium skillet over medium-high heat. Carefully add the garlic slices and cook, stirring continuously, for 2 to 3 minutes, until they begin to brown and become crispy. Transfer with a slotted spoon to the towel-lined plate and sprinkle with the salt.

3. Add the remaining 1 teaspoon minced garlic to the hot oil left in the pan from the garlic chips. Sauté for 30 seconds to 1 minute, until the garlic is fragrant. Then carefully add the marinated shrimp and sauté for 3 to 5 minutes, until all of the shrimp has just barely turned pink.

4. Transfer the shrimp to a wide-rimmed bowl or deep platter. Sprinkle with the parsley and garlic chips and serve immediately.

Switch It Up!

MORE WAYS TO SERVE GARLIC SHRIMP

With diced tomatoes and pasta | With baby greens and lemon juice | Over polenta | With orange segments, shaved fennel, and cherry tomatoes

Roasted Cauliflower
and Radicchio with
White Bean Spread,
page 80

Small Meals

Though sometimes a cook wants to
get creative in the kitchen,
there are definitely times when
all we want for dinner
is a quick, flavorful, satisfying meal without
a lot of fuss or cleanup.
The recipes here have everything
you need in one dish.
Just add a salad and the meal is complete.
The point is that putting healthy,
homemade food on the table isn't tough to do.

SEARED TOMATO, AVOCADO, AND FARMER'S CHEESE TOAST

Although many small kitchens don't have a toaster, there's no need to go without one of life's most comforting pleasures: toast. If you have enough space for a toaster, by all means use it. But there are alternative methods to creating crispy, crunchy bread, like using your oven, an open flame, or even a cast-iron skillet (see page 67) on your stovetop.

Toast piled with delicious toppings can be a quick all-in-one meal. In this particular iteration, you get protein from the cheese and eggs plus the nutritious additions of tomatoes and avocado. Farmer's cheese is a fresh, cow's milk cheese similar to fresh chèvre, but feel free to go rogue! Ricotta, Greek yogurt, or chèvre will all work wonderfully. With toast, the possibilities are limitless.

Serves 1

- 1 teaspoon avocado oil
- ½ tomato, sliced into 4 slices
- Kosher salt and freshly ground black pepper
- 1 slice whole-grain or seedy bread
- 2 tablespoons farmer's cheese
- ½ avocado, sliced
- Squirt of Sriracha (optional)
- 1 or 2 eggs (depending on how hungry you are)

1. Heat the oil in a small skillet over medium-high heat. Add the tomato slices and sprinkle with salt and pepper. Sear on each side until they begin to brown, about 4 minutes per side.

2. Toast the bread and spread with the farmer's cheese. Top with the seared tomato, sliced avocado, a sprinkle of salt, and a squirt of Sriracha, if desired.

3. Heat the same skillet over medium-high heat. Crack the egg(s) into the skillet, sprinkle with salt and pepper, and cover. Fry for 2 to 3 minutes, depending on how you prefer them: 2 minutes for sunny-side up and 3 minutes for over easy. Slide the egg(s) on top of the avocado slices and serve immediately.

Toast in a Skillet

Most of us in small spaces don't have or need a toaster. This mono-tool would otherwise sit and take up space on our precious real estate (countertop). But if you love the smell and flavor of caramelized bread (toast) in the morning, take heart—no toaster is required.

For dry toast, heat a skillet over medium heat, then add the bread. Cook for 3 to 4 minutes per side, and voilà! If you'd like to drizzle a little olive oil or get that delicious toasted-butter crust, add those things to the skillet before the bread goes in.

To then swank up an already lovely invention, top your toast with nut butter, banana, honey, chia seeds, flax seeds, apple slices, or anything else your happy heart desires, whether it's breakfast, lunch, or dinner. Here are some combinations to try:

— Banana, honey, and chia seeds on almond butter

— Apple, maple syrup, and flax seeds on cashew butter

— Melted cheddar with apple slices and walnuts

— Chèvre, walnuts, and olives with roasted red peppers

— Cured salmon with cream cheese, cucumbers, and lemon

— Hummus, grated carrot, and spinach sprinkled with smoked paprika

— Beets, chèvre, and toasted pecans drizzled with lemon juice and extra-virgin olive oil

AVOCADO, ARUGULA, AND SESAME TOAST

Toast is an opportunity to have a little slice of fancy without too much fuss. It's all about the garnish. Furikake, which can be found in the Asian section of most grocery stores these days, is a blend of seaweed and sesame seeds, and just a warning, it's addictive. But you could also try this toast with kimchi and cilantro, with roasted cauliflower and dukkah (page 52), or with seared zucchini and tapenade. Switch it up, and each time you've got another complete and delicious meal.

Serves 1

1 slice whole-grain or seedy bread

½ avocado, mashed

1 cup lightly packed arugula

Sesame oil

Squeeze of fresh lime juice

½ teaspoon furikake

1 or 2 eggs (depending on how hungry you are)

Kosher salt and freshly ground black pepper

1. Toast the bread and spread with the avocado. Top with the arugula and drizzle with sesame oil and lime juice. Sprinkle with furikake.

2. Heat a drizzle of sesame oil in a small skillet over medium-high heat. Crack the egg(s) into the skillet, sprinkle with salt and pepper, and cover. Fry for 2 to 3 minutes, depending on how you prefer them: 2 minutes for sunny-side up and 3 minutes for over easy. Slide the egg(s) on top of the arugula and serve immediately.

GROWN-UP CREAM OF MUSHROOM ON TOAST

When I was growing up, my mom would make cream of mushroom on toast on those nights when she and my dad were heading out for a date. That was the only time she would make it, and my brothers and I all ate our own body's weight of it, and then some, because we loved it so much. This is the grown-up version of that childhood favorite. The sherry adds a tang that sends it into another dimension. Using chicken broth instead of water and cremini or shiitakes instead of button mushrooms gives it a bump of flavor, too.

Serves 2

1½ tablespoons extra-virgin olive oil

10 ounces cremini mushrooms, or an assortment of mushrooms, broken into ¾-inch pieces

Pinch of kosher salt

Several grinds of black pepper

½ cup heavy cream

¼ cup dry sherry

¼ cup water or chicken broth

⅓ of a baguette

1. Heat the oil in a large skillet over high heat. Add the mushrooms, salt, and pepper and sauté until the mushrooms have all browned, 5 to 7 minutes. (Be sure the skillet is big enough that the juice from the mushrooms can evaporate and the skillet can develop a brown film.)

2. Add the heavy cream, sherry, and water to the skillet and bring to a boil. Use a wooden spoon to loosen any browned bits from the bottom of the skillet. The sauce should be slightly thickened but still pourable.

3. Tear the piece of baguette in half and then tear each half open, creating four open-faced pieces. Toast them slightly to warm.

4. Spoon the mushroom sauce on top of the toasted baguette and serve.

Switch It Up!

MORE WAYS TO USE CREAM OF MUSHROOM SAUCE

On steak or chicken | Over polenta | With pasta

ROASTED RED BELL PEPPER HALVES
WITH LINGUIÇA AND FETA

While the happy colors of red peppers and yellow tomatoes pop against the white of the feta, this dish allows for endless variation. Try fennel sausage topped with Parmesan cheese or prosciutto topped with chèvre. The feta is salty and so is the sausage, but even so, a little dusting of salt on the tomatoes makes the whole dish sing.

Serves 2

- 2 red bell peppers, cut in half and seeds removed
- 5 ounces linguiça sausage, cut into ¼-inch slices
- 4 ounces feta cheese, sliced into 4 pieces
- 6 golden (or red) cherry tomatoes, cut in half
- 2 teaspoons extra-virgin olive oil
- Pinch of kosher salt

1. Preheat the oven to 400°F (200°C).

2. Place the pepper halves in a roasting pan or pie plate, cut side facing up. Fill the pepper halves with sausage. Place a feta slice on top of the sausage, followed by the tomato halves. Drizzle with the olive oil and sprinkle sparingly with salt.

3. Roast for 1 hour and 10 minutes, or until the peppers are soft and beginning to brown on the edges.

CRAB AND AVOCADO CRÊPES WITH CHIPOTLE CREAM

Crêpes are like skinny pancakes and just as simple to make. They can be made savory or sweet and can serve as a snack or a meal.

When our girls were little, we'd occasionally have a snow day from school. After some serious snowlady making, crêpes were often on the menu. The girls would "help" me make the batter, and as they got older it became a badge of pride for them to be able to successfully flip the crêpes in the small skillet. When they were all made, we'd spread them with Nutella and have them with tea. It couldn't have been more delightful.

If you don't have this exact group of filling ingredients and are looking to make a meal, see page 40 for some other ideas on how to use up little bits of this and that for your crêpes.

Serves 2; makes 4 crêpes

CRÊPES

½ cup plus 2 tablespoons all-purpose flour

2 large eggs

½ cup plus 2 tablespoons cold water

½ cup milk

1½ tablespoons unsalted butter, melted, plus a dab for the skillet

Pinch of kosher salt

CHIPOTLE CREAM

¼ cup heavy cream

2 teaspoons fresh lemon juice

1 teaspoon finely minced chipotle en adobo

Pinch of kosher salt

FILLING

½ tablespoon salted butter

4 ounces crabmeat (about ½ cup)

½ avocado, sliced

4 poached eggs (optional; see page 77)

Pinch of kosher salt

Recipe continues on next page

1. Preheat the oven to its lowest setting. Set a plate or platter in the oven to warm.

2. To make the crêpe batter, whisk the flour, eggs, water, milk, melted butter, and salt together in a medium bowl. Refrigerate for at least 30 minutes.

3. Heat a small nonstick skillet over medium heat for 3 minutes, or until it's hot. Then add a dab of butter, let it melt, and ladle ¼ cup of the crêpe batter into the skillet. Tilt the skillet to coat the bottom. After 30 seconds to a minute, when you can see that bubbles have formed, flip it and cook until it's just beginning to brown, another 30 seconds to 1 minute. Transfer the finished crêpe to the plate in the warm oven. (Don't worry if the first crêpe is a loss; it usually is. The next ones will be fine. You shouldn't need butter after the first crêpe.)

4. To make the chipotle cream, combine the cream, lemon juice, chipotle, and salt in a small skillet and bring to a boil over high heat. Pour the sauce into a small cup or pitcher and set aside for serving.

5. To assemble the crêpes, melt the butter in the same small skillet and add the crabmeat to warm it up. Layer crabmeat, avocado, and a poached egg, if you're using them, on each crêpe and roll them up. Set the crêpes seam side down on plates, drizzle with the chipotle cream, and serve immediately.

Switch It Up!

MORE WAYS TO USE CHIPOTLE CREAM

With wilted spinach | In scrambled eggs | As a spread on a pork sandwich with avocado and greens | With roasted vegetables

PAN-SEARED ITALIAN VEGETABLES WITH FRIED CAPERS, OLIVES, AND BURRATA

This dish is so satisfying that, with some crusty bread dipped in olive oil, it can stand on its own as a main dish. In the winter we pan-sear the veggies, and in the summer we grill them. Either way, we always fry the capers and the olives to boost the flavor and give the dish a tiny bit of crispy texture. Of course, the dish is also lovely as a side to some grilled chicken or seared pork tenderloin, in which case it would serve closer to four people.

Serves 2

Extra-virgin olive oil

½ fennel bulb, cut into ¾-inch wedges

1 red onion, cut into ¾-inch wedges

2 medium zucchinis, sliced diagonally into ½-inch rounds

8 ounces sweet mini peppers (about 14 peppers)

Kosher salt and freshly ground black pepper

2 balls fresh burrata cheese (3 to 4 ounces each)

4 tablespoons capers

6 Castelvetrano olives, pitted and broken in half

1. Heat 1 tablespoon of oil in a large skillet over medium-high heat. Add the fennel, onions, zucchini, and peppers in a single layer. Sprinkle with salt and pepper, and sear until the vegetables become golden brown and tender, about 10 minutes. It may take more than one round to cook all of the vegetables. Each time, add a little oil to the skillet and sprinkle with salt and pepper.

2. When the vegetables are cooked, transfer them to a platter. Tear up the burrata and scatter the pieces on top of the hot vegetables.

3. Add a drizzle of oil to the skillet and fry the capers and olives until they get a little crispy, 30 seconds to 1 minute. Spoon them on top of the vegetables and burrata and serve.

How to Poach Eggs

Eggs are a magical food, easy to make and packed with nutrition. And could they be more delicious? To my mind, adding a poached egg to most any meal makes it a perfect one. Once you master the technique of poaching, the possibilities are endless. A word to the wise: Use the freshest eggs you can find for poaching. The fresher they are, the better they hold together while cooking.

1. To poach about 4 eggs at a time, fill a large saucepan with at least 2 inches of water. Add ½ teaspoon kosher salt and 1 teaspoon of white vinegar and bring almost to a simmer over high heat. Then reduce the heat so that the water is just barely burping.

2. Use a wooden spoon to gently swirl the water in one direction. Carefully crack each egg into the center of the pan, bringing the eggs as close to the surface as possible before releasing them into the water. If this is difficult, crack each egg into a cup, then lower the cup's edge to the surface of the water and gently slip the egg into the water. Ever so gently swirl the water again in the same direction. If it looks like the whites are going to trail around the yolks in wisps, agitate the water next to each egg, again ever so gently, to help them hold together.

3. Just barely simmer the eggs for 4 to 5 minutes, depending on how loose you like your yolks. You can tell that an egg is done when you lift it out of the water and the center is still jiggly but the white is firm. Remove the eggs with a slotted spoon, dabbing the bottom of the spoon on a towel to remove excess water.

POTATOES AND BROKEN EGGS WITH SPINACH AND SMOKED PAPRIKA

The yolks in this dish are meant to be broken, which is why we add them to the skillet from a little height. The idea comes from a Spanish dish called huevos rotos (broken eggs), and I added spinach because, well, greens make everything healthier. This is a perfect weeknight meal or late-morning weekend brunch for two.

Serves 2

- 3 tablespoons extra-virgin olive oil
- 1 pound baby potatoes, halved
- 2 cups sliced onion (about 1 large onion)
- 2 cloves garlic, smashed

  Kosher salt
- ¼ teaspoon smoked paprika

  Dash of red pepper flakes
- 3 cups lightly packed baby spinach
- 2–4 eggs (depending on how hungry you are)

1. Heat the oil in a medium skillet over medium-high heat. Add the potatoes, onion, garlic, ¾ teaspoon salt, paprika, and red pepper flakes and cover with a lid. Move the potatoes and onions around occasionally with a spatula or by shaking the skillet. When the potatoes begin to brown, reduce the heat to medium-low and cook, covered, until the potatoes are tender when pierced with a fork, 15 to 20 minutes.

2. Add the spinach and stir gently for 30 seconds.

3. Break the eggs into the skillet from a height of about 12 inches, sprinkle with a pinch of salt, and cover. Let cook for 2 to 3 minutes, until the whites are cooked through. Serve in the skillet immediately.

KALE, SWEET POTATO, AND CARAMELIZED SHALLOTS WITH YOGURT TAHINI SAUCE

This combination of kale, sweet potatoes, and caramelized shallots is so satisfying that it's easy to forget this dish is vegetarian. And while the yogurt tahini sauce is great on these vegetables, it could also be drizzled on, well, almost anything. As an added bonus, the entire recipe uses only one pan, plus one small bowl for the sauce.

Serves 2

Extra-virgin olive oil

½ cup thinly sliced shallots (about 2 shallots)

Kosher salt and freshly ground black pepper

1 large sweet potato, cut into 6 lengthwise slices about ¼ inch wide

4 ounces kale, coarsely chopped (about 1 small bunch or 4 cups)

YOGURT TAHINI SAUCE

⅓ cup low-fat or whole-milk plain yogurt

2 tablespoons tahini

2 teaspoons fresh lemon juice

2 teaspoons tamari

½ teaspoon minced garlic (about ½ clove)

1. Heat 1 tablespoon oil in a medium skillet over medium-low heat. Add the shallots, sprinkle with salt and pepper, and sauté for 7 to 10 minutes, until the shallots are caramelized. Transfer the shallots to a small bowl and set aside.

2. Drizzle a little more oil in the skillet. Add the sweet potatoes, sprinkle with salt and pepper, and cook, turning the slices occasionally, for about 20 minutes, until they are nicely browned and tender.

3. Meanwhile, make the yogurt tahini sauce: Whisk the yogurt, tahini, lemon juice, tamari, and garlic together in a small bowl.

4. When the sweet potatoes are tender, remove them from the skillet and set aside. Turn up the heat to medium-high and add the kale. Drizzle with a little more oil, sprinkle with salt and pepper, and sauté for 4 to 5 minutes, until the kale is tender but still bright green.

5. Transfer the kale to a platter. Top with the sweet potatoes, drizzle with the yogurt sauce, and finish with the shallots. Serve with extra sauce.

Switch It Up!

MORE WAYS TO USE YOGURT TAHINI SAUCE

Over steamed veggies | With baked potato and spinach | As a salad dressing | With everything

ROASTED CAULIFLOWER AND RADICCHIO WITH WHITE BEAN SPREAD

Something magical happens when cauliflower is roasted. It is, hands down, my favorite way to cook cauliflower and by far the easiest. The slightly bitter radicchio sits just right alongside the sweetness of the cauliflower and the bean spread.

Serves 2

1 small head cauliflower, cut into small florets (about 5 cups)

½ head radicchio, cored and cut into ½-inch wedges

2 tablespoons extra-virgin olive oil

Kosher salt and freshly ground black pepper

WHITE BEAN SPREAD (MAKES 2 CUPS)

1 (15-ounce) can cannellini beans, drained

½ cup tahini

3 tablespoons fresh lemon juice (from about 1 lemon)

2 tablespoons tamari

1 tablespoon extra-virgin olive oil

1 clove garlic, minced

Freshly ground black pepper

1. Preheat the oven to 375°F (190°C).

2. Line a baking pan with parchment. Lay the cauliflower on half of the pan and the radicchio on the other half. The radicchio may not all stay together; that's fine. Drizzle with the oil and sprinkle with salt and pepper. Roast for 20 minutes, or until the radicchio begins to brown. Remove the radicchio from the pan and continue roasting the cauliflower for another 25 to 30 minutes, until browned on the outside and tender on the inside.

3. Make the bean spread: Mash the beans with a fork or potato masher in a small bowl. Add the tahini, lemon juice, tamari, oil, garlic, and several grinds of black pepper and mix well. Alternatively, pulse the ingredients in a small food processor until smooth.

4. To serve, smooth the bean spread onto a serving platter and top with the roasted cauliflower and radicchio.

Switch It Up!

MORE WAYS TO USE WHITE BEAN SPREAD

With pita chips | On toast with wilted spinach and feta | With olives and almonds as an appetizer | Swirled into a vegetable soup

CUCUMBER, WALNUT, AND YOGURT SOUP

This bright soup is elegant enough for a summer appetizer al fresco and hearty enough to be a super-quick weeknight meal. Pair it with crispy homemade crackers or maybe seared scallops over delicate greens drizzled with a dressing of mint, basil, olive oil, and lemon.

Serves 2

2 cups peeled, seeded, and coarsely chopped cucumber (about 2 cucumbers)

½ cup chicken broth

½ cup low-fat or whole-milk plain yogurt

¼ cup walnuts

2 tablespoons fresh lemon juice (from about ½ lemon)

1 tablespoon extra-virgin olive oil, plus extra for garnish

2 tablespoons fresh dill, plus extra for garnish

2 tablespoons fresh mint, plus extra for garnish

2 tablespoons minced scallions, plus extra for garnish

Fat pinch of kosher salt

Dash of Tabasco or Cholula sauce

1. Combine cucumbers, broth, yogurt, walnuts, lemon juice, olive oil, dill, mint, scallions, salt, and Tabasco in a blender (or use an immersion blender) and blend well. Taste the soup, and adjust the seasoning with drops of lemon juice, small pinches of salt, or little dashes of hot sauce if needed.

2. Serve chilled, garnished with dill, mint, scallions, and a drizzle of olive oil.

SWISS CHARD WITH PINE NUT "CREAM"

Now, the word *cream* is in this recipe's name, and a glug or two of fresh cream wouldn't be amiss here at all. However, this lovely sauce has a creamy flavor all its own without the use of any actual cream. It offers a burst of toasty, salty goodness and stands up nicely to the slight stout bitterness of the greens. If you don't have a food processor, don't fret—it will have a little more texture but will be just as wonderful. And don't let the anchovies scare you. One of our testers made this for her sister who hates them, and she couldn't even recognize they were there.

Serves 2

SWISS CHARD

- 1 tablespoon extra-virgin olive oil
- 1 bunch Swiss chard, chopped, with thick stems separated from leaves (about 8 cups lightly packed)
- ¼ cup thinly sliced shallots (about 1 shallot)

  Kosher salt and freshly ground black pepper

PINE NUT CREAM (MAKES ¾ CUP)

- ½ cup pine nuts
- 2 tablespoons anchovies in oil
- 2 tablespoons fresh flat-leaf parsley
- ½ clove garlic
- 2 tablespoons extra-virgin olive oil
- 1 teaspoon fresh lemon juice

  Freshly ground black pepper

1. Heat the oil in a medium skillet over medium-high heat. Add the chopped chard stems, shallots, a tiny pinch of salt, and a few grinds of pepper. Go easy here with the salt, as the anchovies are salty and will give that flavor to the greens. Sauté for 7 to 10 minutes, until the shallots are translucent.

2. Add the chard leaves, another tiny pinch of salt and a few grinds of pepper, and sauté, turning the chard with tongs occasionally, for 4 to 5 minutes, until the greens are fully cooked.

3. To make the pine nut cream, mince the nuts, anchovies, parsley, and garlic and combine with the olive oil, lemon juice, and a few grinds of pepper in a small bowl. Alternatively, pulse all the ingredients in a food processor.

4. To serve, lay the Swiss chard on a platter and dot with the pine nut cream.

Switch It Up!
MORE WAYS TO USE PINE NUT CREAM

With grilled chicken | With seared asparagus or green beans | Spread on toast with sliced tomatoes and olive oil | Tossed with pasta, baby spinach, and a dash of heavy cream

ASPARAGUS AND TOMATO GRATIN

This one-pan dish can either be a meal on its own or play a supporting role as a side dish. Most of the time, in our household, we serve it with a green salad and some fresh bread as dinner. When I make it in a cast-iron skillet, the skillet becomes the serving platter so that we have one less dish to wash at the end of the meal.

Vegetables that could be substituted for the asparagus include eggplant, zucchini, and summer squash. You could also replace the thyme with rosemary, sage, or even spices like cumin or smoked paprika.

Serves 2

¼ cup fresh (or panko) bread crumbs

1½ tablespoons extra-virgin olive oil

½ teaspoon fresh thyme

¼ cup grated Asiago cheese

1 bunch asparagus, cut into 3-inch lengths

Salt and freshly ground black pepper

1 tomato, diced (about 1 cup)

1. Heat a small skillet over medium heat and add the bread crumbs. Toast for 2 to 3 minutes, until they become golden brown. Add 1 tablespoon of the oil along with the thyme, stir to combine, and then stir in the cheese. Transfer to a small bowl and return the skillet to the heat.

2. Heat the remaining ½ tablespoon oil in the same skillet over medium-high heat. Add the asparagus, season with the salt and pepper, and sauté for 4 to 5 minutes, until the asparagus begins to sear on the outside.

3. Add the tomatoes and sprinkle with a little more salt. Cook until the asparagus is tender, another 1 to 3 minutes, depending on how thick the spears are. Then transfer the vegetables to a serving platter and top with the bread crumbs.

AVOCADO CITRUS SOUP

The idea for this recipe originated with my friend Betsy Maislen, who has sailed with us as an assistant in my galley at the end of the season, when the cook's creativity begins to ebb. Betsy marches in and starts throwing out ideas that we run with over and over again. She always brings a wonderful breath of fresh vitality and creativity.

    This healthy, refreshing chilled soup is a beauty on hot days when no one wants to get near the stove. No equipment is necessary except your knife and a cutting board. It's like summertime served in a bowl.

Serves 2

½ cup minced onion (about 1 small onion)

½ teaspoon kosher salt

1 avocado, finely diced

1 plum tomato, finely diced (about ¾ cup)

2 teaspoons grated lemon zest
   (from about 1 lemon)

1 teaspoon grated lime zest
   (from about ½ lime)

1 teaspoon minced garlic (about 1 clove)

2 cups good-quality orange juice

⅓ cup fresh lemon and lime juice
   (from about 1 lemon and 1 lime)

1 tablespoon extra-virgin olive oil

2 tablespoons minced fresh cilantro,
   for garnish

1. Combine the onion and salt in a small bowl, mix well, and set aside for 20 to 30 minutes. Drain any liquid.

2. Combine the onions with the avocado, tomato, lemon zest, lime zest, and garlic in a quart jar or medium bowl. Pour in the orange juice, lemon and lime juice, and olive oil and mix well.

3. Chill for at least 1 hour. Serve cold, garnished with cilantro.

CHAPTER 5

SALADS AND ONE-BOWL MAINS

In a tiny kitchen, building an entire meal in just one bowl
is a simple way to reduce the number of dirty dishes.
When you are hosting a crowd, serving bowls
plus dinnerware may be necessary, but when you have
only one or two people, there's no real need
to do the family-style thing. That said, if
I've gone to the trouble of creating a beautiful meal,
I like to take a minute to make everything
look appealing before the serving begins.
I also like to set the table, light a candle, use cloth napkins,
and generally have mealtime be an oasis
from the rest of the day. For a moment,
we can sit and look each other in the eyes and say,
"Nice to be in the same room with you."
And maybe even say a prayer of thanks or speak out loud
the things for which we are grateful.

Starring: The Salad

Salads are fine in a supporting role,
but I like them best as the main event.
Lots of greens, protein, cheese, something crunchy—
add a couple of punches of flavor,
and I'm a happy girl.
Salad is a perfect meal for a tiny kitchen,
since it can often be built on a platter
or in a bowl. Very few dirty dishes ensue,
and a healthy meal is still the result.

BUTTERMILK FRIED CHICKEN SALAD
WITH APPLES AND BLUE CHEESE

Could we just call this the grown-up version of fried chicken and concede that a salad is a good idea for healthy living, but we don't want to completely forgo the decadent things in life? Some of those decadent things are just pure pleasure, and that's what this salad is: crispy fried chicken, sweet crunchy apples, and tangy, creamy blue cheese, all on a bed of greens.

Look for chicken breasts that are not more than about ¾ inch thick to allow for appropriate cooking times.

Serves 2

FRIED CHICKEN
- ½ cup buttermilk
- 1 clove garlic, smashed
- ½ teaspoon kosher salt, plus a pinch for the dredging flour
- ½ teaspoon Tabasco Chipotle Pepper Sauce
- ¼ teaspoon paprika, plus a pinch for the dredging flour
- 2 boneless chicken breasts (about 6 ounces each)
- 1 cup peanut or canola oil
- ¼ cup all-purpose flour

BUTTERMILK DRESSING
- ¼ cup buttermilk
- 2 tablespoons mayonnaise
- 1 teaspoon fresh lemon juice
- ½ teaspoon minced garlic (about ½ clove)
- Kosher salt and freshly ground black pepper

SALAD
- 4 cups lightly packed green leaf lettuce
- ½ apple, thinly sliced
- 1 rib celery, thinly sliced
- ¼ fennel bulb, thinly sliced
- 2 ounces crumbled blue cheese (about ½ cup)

Recipe continues on next page

1. To make the chicken, mix the buttermilk, garlic, salt, Tabasco, and paprika in a medium bowl, and then submerge the chicken in the mixture. Use at once, or refrigerate for up to 24 hours.

2. Heat the peanut oil to 375°F (190°C) in a high-sided skillet over medium heat. Mix the flour with a pinch of salt and a pinch of paprika and spread on a plate.

3. Dredge the chicken in the flour mixture and carefully lay the breasts in the hot oil. Cook for 4 to 5 minutes on each side, or until an instant-read thermometer registers an internal temperature of 160°F (70°C).

4. To make the dressing, combine the buttermilk, mayonnaise, lemon juice, garlic, a pinch of salt, and several grinds of pepper in a small bowl. Mix well.

5. To assemble the salad, lay the lettuce on a serving platter or two plates. Arrange the apple, celery, and fennel over the lettuce. Drizzle the dressing over the vegetables and top with the blue cheese. Slice the chicken breasts diagonally into ¼-inch slices and lay on top.

TUNA, GRAPEFRUIT, AND AVOCADO CEVICHE WITH PICKLED JALAPEÑO

This freshest of fresh meals is packed with protein and filled with flavor. I began to love ceviche while cooking in the Caribbean islands, and my love has never really waned. If you want to go for an Asian rather than Latin American flavor, substitute a red Thai chile for the jalapeño pepper, rice wine vinegar instead of apple cider vinegar, tamari in place of salt, and sesame oil instead of avocado oil. Sprinkle with sesame seeds.

This method of quick pickling the jalapeños can be done with almost any chile or vegetable and adds another layer of flavor and depth to any dish (see page 97 for more quick-pickling tips).

Fresh tuna is a must with this recipe. Purchase from a local fishmonger whom you trust.

Serves 2 as a main course or 4 as an appetizer

1 jalapeño pepper, very thinly sliced

Kosher salt

2 tablespoons apple cider vinegar

3 cups pea shoots

5 ounces sashimi-grade tuna, thinly sliced

1 grapefruit, segmented

½ avocado, thinly sliced

½ cup diced mango

2 tablespoons avocado oil

1. Toss the jalapeño slices with a pinch of salt in a small bowl and let sit for at least 5 minutes. Add the vinegar, stir, and set aside.

2. Arrange the pea shoots on a platter and dot with the tuna, grapefruit, avocado, and mango. Drizzle with the avocado oil and the vinegar from the pickled jalapeños, and sprinkle with salt. Garnish with the jalapeños and serve immediately.

Quick Pickling

My earliest memory of pickles is of walking into my grandma's kitchen after a summer afternoon spent wandering in the fields and gardens behind her house, picking Queen Anne's lace and climbing trees. Coming in from the fresh air to a kitchen filled with the powerful scent of vinegar was like running into a sensory wall.

As I've gotten older, I've come to appreciate foods with stronger smells and tastes, with sharply vinegary pickles among them. However, making pickles—prepping, filling, canning, and boiling—can be involved, and there's something to be said for a simpler, less time-consuming process. It's called the "quick pickle," and almost every culture on the planet has a version of this very simple technique. And rightly so, as these little babies pack a wonderful punch and add zing to a meal.

Quick pickling is easy, and I use it often when I have a vegetable that I need to use up.

1. Slice, julienne, chop, or dice the vegetable.

2. Sprinkle with sea salt and toss. Let sit for at least 5 minutes and up to overnight.

3. Add vinegar of any kind and herbs, as well as spices, onions, chiles, and/or mustard seeds.

4. Serve immediately or refrigerate for later.

CANNELLINI BEAN, TUNA, AND BRIE SALAD

A number of years ago, my friend Emily Strauss, a cookbook author herself, came in from Boston to sail with us. While we were down at the boat greeting guests, she made this salad for our girls. It was such a hit that it became a standard in our house. Because it's so simple, the quality of the tuna matters greatly. Whether it's packed in oil or water is more preference than requirement.

Serves 2

1 baby head Boston, Bibb, or some other tender lettuce

1 tomato, cut into ¾-inch wedges

Grated zest from ½ lemon

2 tablespoons fresh lemon juice (from about ½ lemon)

1 tablespoon extra-virgin olive oil

Kosher salt and freshly ground black pepper

1 cup canned cannellini beans, rinsed and drained

1 (5-ounce) can good-quality tuna, well drained

1 ounce Brie cheese, torn into pieces

1. Arrange the lettuce leaves on a serving platter or two plates.

2. Arrange the tomato on top. Scatter the lemon zest over the top, drizzle with the lemon juice and oil and sprinkle with salt and pepper.

3. Arrange the beans, tuna, and Brie on top and serve.

AVOCADO, RADISH, AND TOASTED SUNFLOWER SEEDS WITH LEMON

This salad is the simplest of dishes, but one I turn to over and over again in midwinter or spring, when the grocery-store tomatoes and cucumbers are insipid and the garden varieties seem endlessly far away. I take great joy in discovering fresh radishes and baby heads of lettuce at our indoor farmers' market in the off-season, filling me with gratitude for all the farmers who grow under a greenhouse. When the heads are so beautiful and fresh, I've taken to using the greens whole. I simply wash and dry the heads well, lop off the root end, and splay the leaves whole on a platter, arranging all the adornments on top.

Serves 2

1 head baby lettuce (about 5 ounces)

4 radishes, quartered

½ avocado

1 tablespoon extra-virgin olive oil

2 teaspoons fresh lemon juice

Kosher salt and freshly ground black pepper

2 tablespoons toasted, salted sunflower seeds

1. Lay the baby lettuce leaves out on a platter. Top with the radishes. Scoop out pieces of avocado with a small spoon and dot them onto the lettuce leaves.

2. Drizzle the salad with oil and lemon juice and sprinkle with salt and pepper. Scatter the sunflower seeds on top and serve immediately.

GRAPEFRUIT, SEA-SALTED SPICED WALNUTS, AND ARUGULA SALAD

To make this a delicious dinner, add some pan-seared salmon or some slices of pork tenderloin. This recipe makes more sea-salted spiced walnuts than are required, but why wouldn't you want more? Just store the leftovers in an airtight container. They are so good, I dare you to try to save them for more than a day.

Serves 2

SEA-SALTED SPICED WALNUTS (MAKES 2 CUPS)

2 teaspoons honey

1 teaspoon extra-virgin olive oil

½ teaspoon ground allspice

½ teaspoon ground cumin

3 tablespoons sugar

Sea salt and freshly ground black pepper

2 cups walnuts

SALAD

4 cups lightly packed arugula

1 tablespoon avocado oil

1 teaspoon fresh lemon juice

Kosher salt and freshly ground black pepper

1 grapefruit, segmented

3 tablespoons pomegranate seeds

¼ cup sea-salted spiced walnuts

1. To make the spiced walnuts, heat the honey and olive oil in a small skillet over medium-high heat. Stir in the allspice and cumin. Add the sugar, along with a fat pinch of sea salt and several grinds of pepper. Dribble a tiny bit of water into the center of the skillet to encourage the sugar to melt. As soon as the mixture is bubbling, turn off the heat and add the walnuts. Stir well, breaking up any clumps, until the walnuts all have a little sugar on them. Transfer to a plate to cool.

2. To make the salad, arrange the arugula on a serving platter or in bowls. Drizzle with the avocado oil and lemon juice and sprinkle with salt and pepper. Arrange the grapefruit segments on top and scatter the pomegranate seeds and walnuts over everything.

Switch It Up!

MORE WAYS TO USE SEA-SALTED SPICED WALNUTS

With yogurt and berries | On pizza with caramelized onions and Gorgonzola | With kale and raisins | On their own as a snack

BABY POTATO, WATERCRESS, AND RADISH SALAD WITH CREAMY GARLIC AND DILL DRIZZLE

Potatoes are the underappreciated laborers of the kitchen, but they can also be elegant guests at your table. Here, they are a little of both, one of the reasons I love them so.

Garden-fresh radishes have a ton of flavor but are only available during some parts of the year. If yours must come from the grocery store, as mine often do in Maine, toss them with a little salt and lemon juice and let them sit for 10 minutes or so to ease the sharp, peppery bite.

Serves 2 as a meal or 4 as a side dish

SALAD

- 12 ounces red baby potatoes (about 20 potatoes)

  Kosher salt

- 2 tablespoons extra-virgin olive oil

- 1 teaspoon fresh lemon juice

- 3 ounces watercress (about 4 cups lightly packed)

- 5 radishes, thinly sliced

CREAMY GARLIC AND DILL DRIZZLE

- ¼ cup buttermilk

- 2 tablespoons sour cream

- 1 tablespoon minced fresh dill, plus extra for garnish

- ½ teaspoon minced garlic (about ½ clove)

  Squeeze of fresh lemon juice

  Kosher salt and freshly ground black pepper

1. Make the drizzle: Whisk the buttermilk, sour cream, dill, garlic, lemon juice, a pinch of salt, and several grinds of pepper together in a small bowl.

2. Put the potatoes in a medium stockpot, add enough water to cover them, and salt it well. Bring to a boil over high heat. Boil until tender, about 10 minutes, then drain.

3. When the potatoes are cool enough to handle, cut them in half and transfer to a large bowl. Toss with a pinch of salt, the oil, and the lemon juice.

4. Arrange the potatoes with the watercress and radish slices on a platter or two plates. Drizzle the dressing over the salad in a spiral motion.

Switch It Up!

MORE WAYS TO USE CREAMY GARLIC AND DILL DRIZZLE

Over steamed green beans with walnuts | Thickened with mayonnaise and served as a dip | Over kale with croutons | As a spread for salmon burgers

CARROT, BEET, AND APPLE SALAD WITH GINGER, LIME, AND CILANTRO

There are two ways to make this recipe. One is with a mandolin, which slices the veggies and the apple super thin and makes an elegant presentation. If you don't have a mandolin, no worries, the other method is with a grater and also works beautifully. Keep everything separate until serving time as the beets tend to stain the carrots and the apples quickly.

Carrots that come fresh from a farmers' market or garden don't need to be peeled; their skin will be tender and sweet. Scrubbing them takes off just a light layer and leaves them glowing with color.

Serves 2

1 Honey Crisp or other tart apple

1 small beet

1 large carrot

Extra-virgin olive oil

Grated zest and juice of 1 lime

Kosher salt and freshly ground black pepper

Grated fresh ginger

Fresh cilantro, for garnish

1. Use a mandolin or grater to slice or grate the apple, beet, and carrot as thinly as possible.

2. Layer all three on a wide platter. Drizzle with the oil and lime juice and sprinkle with salt and pepper. Sprinkle the lime zest and grate the ginger onto the sliced vegetables to taste. Garnish with cilantro and serve immediately.

WATERMELON, CUCUMBER, FETA, AND MINT SALAD

With this salad, the colder the ingredients, the better, especially in the middle of summer when a salad to beat the heat is just the thing. The combination of sweet, juicy watermelon, crisp cucumber, and salty feta strikes a perfect note. I like to serve this salad with grilled chicken marinated with lime and garlic or with pork rubbed with a jerk seasoning.

Serves 2

SALAD

2 ounces watermelon, cut into thin, bite-size triangles (about 2 cups)

6 baby cucumbers, thinly sliced (about 1 cup)

2 radishes, thinly sliced

4 ounces feta cheese, cut into ½-inch cubes (about ½ cup)

¼ cup coarsely chopped fresh mint

DRESSING

2 tablespoons brine from the feta (or a fat pinch of kosher salt)

2 tablespoons white balsamic vinegar

1 tablespoon extra-virgin olive oil

½ teaspoon grated lime zest

1 tablespoon fresh lime juice (from about ½ lime)

1 teaspoon grated fresh ginger

1. To prepare the salad, combine the watermelon, cucumbers, radishes, feta, and mint in a large bowl.

2. To make the dressing, whisk the feta brine, vinegar, oil, lime zest, lime juice, and ginger together in a small bowl.

3. Gently toss the watermelon mixture with the dressing and serve immediately.

WHITE BALSAMIC SEARED PEACH SALAD WITH BURRATA AND TOASTED ALMONDS

Creamy burrata, mozzarella's elegant cousin, is sublime in this recipe. What a rock-star combination of flavors. The peaches are just as delicious when served uncooked, especially if it's the height of their season.

To turn this dish into an appetizer, omit the lettuce and add wedges of tomato, sliced the same size as the peaches, and serve with crostini.

Serves 2

¼ cup slivered almonds

Kosher salt

1 teaspoon extra-virgin olive oil, plus extra for drizzling

1 peach, thinly sliced

Freshly ground black pepper

1 teaspoon white balsamic vinegar, plus extra for drizzling

1 small head green oak leaf lettuce

2 slices prosciutto

1 (3- to 4-ounce) ball fresh burrata cheese

1. Heat a small skillet over medium-high heat. Add the almonds and cook, stirring continuously, until they begin to brown, 2 to 3 minutes. Transfer immediately to a plate to cool, and sprinkle with salt.

2. Return the skillet to the heat and add the oil. When it's warm, add the peach slices and sprinkle them with salt and pepper. Sear for 2 to 3 minutes, until the edges begin to brown. Add the vinegar and shake the pan to stir, then transfer the seared peaches to a platter to cool slightly.

3. To build the salad, spread whole lettuce leaves out on a platter. Drizzle with oil and vinegar and sprinkle with salt and pepper. Tear the prosciutto into pieces and spread them over the lettuce. Do the same with the burrata. Arrange the peach slices on top and sprinkle with the toasted almonds. Serve immediately.

ENDIVE, ASPARAGUS, AND BLACK FOREST HAM SALAD WITH HORSERADISH DILL DRESSING

The process of building a salad on the platter is easy yet elegant—and perfect for small kitchens, where the fewer dishes you have to wash, the better. Rather than tossing the salad, drizzle the dressing on top to allow the individual ingredients to have their own little spotlight. The result is a beautiful meal to which only bread need be added.

Serves 2

SALAD

2-4 eggs (depending on how hungry you are)

Kosher salt

1 bunch asparagus, cut into 2-inch lengths

1 head Belgian endive

½ cup julienned Black Forest ham

Dill sprigs, for garnish

HORSERADISH DILL DRESSING

¼ cup sour cream

1½ tablespoons prepared horseradish

½ teaspoon fresh lemon juice

2 tablespoons chopped fresh dill

Kosher salt and freshly ground black pepper

1. Put the eggs in a small pot and cover with water. Bring to a boil, then remove the pot from the heat and set a timer for 6 minutes (for soft-boiled). When the timer goes off, transfer the eggs to a bowl of very cold water. When they are cool, remove them from the water, peel them, and cut them in half.

2. Return the pot of water to the heat, add a pinch of salt, and bring to a boil. Add the asparagus and cook for 3 to 4 minutes, until the asparagus is tender but still bright green. Drain and transfer to the bowl of cold water. Drain again and blot with a towel to dry.

3. To make the dressing, whisk the sour cream, horseradish, lemon juice, dill, a pinch of salt, and several grinds of black pepper together in a small bowl.

4. Arrange the endive leaves on a platter and top with the asparagus, ham, and eggs. Drizzle with the dressing and dot with dill sprigs.

GARAM MASALA CHÈVRE WITH ROASTED BELL PEPPER, GREEN BEANS, AND PITA SALAD

This bright, fresh vegetarian meal is inspired by Indian flavors, with deep notes of cardamom, cumin, and allspice. The scent of this meal evokes for me not-yet-made memories of places and people I have yet to see and meet. It's like a promise of a future adventure. This dish is just as nice on a chilly winter night as it is on a warm summer evening.

Serves 2

- 1 red bell pepper
- ½ teaspoon garam masala
- ¼ teaspoon ground cardamom
- ¼ teaspoon ground ginger
- 2 tablespoons extra-virgin olive oil
- 6 ounces fresh green beans (about 1 generous handful)
- ¼ cup chèvre
- 1 head baby romaine
- ¼ cup pitted kalamata olives
- 1 teaspoon fresh lemon juice
  Kosher salt and freshly ground black pepper
- 1 large pita bread, sliced

1. Roast the pepper over a flame, on an electric burner, or in a hot skillet, turning it as the skin blisters. The pepper is done when the whole exterior has blistered and blackened. Remove from the heat and set aside. When cool enough to handle, remove the skin and seeds.

2. Heat a small skillet over medium-high heat and have the garam masala, cardamom, ginger, and oil measured and ready to go. When the skillet is hot, add the spices and stir for 30 seconds, until they just barely begin to smoke. Remove from the heat, add the oil immediately, stir, and then transfer to a small bowl and set aside.

3. Return the skillet to the heat, add the green beans, and cover. Sear the beans until they are tender and a little blistered, about 7 minutes. Remove from the heat.

4. Combine the chèvre and 2 teaspoons of the spiced oil in a small bowl. Mix well.

5. Lay out whole lettuce leaves on a platter and layer with the green beans and olives. Tear the roasted pepper into pieces and layer on top. Drizzle with the rest of the spiced oil and the lemon juice, and sprinkle with salt and pepper. Dot with the chèvre and serve with sliced pita bread.

SEARED ROMAINE WITH CORN, TOMATOES, AND LEMON AIOLI

Aioli—basically homemade mayonnaise—is super easy to make and a wonderful technique to master, drizzling in the oil ever so gradually as you whisk vigorously and then increasing the stream of oil as the sauce begins to thicken. Aioli is a versatile friend to the small kitchen. In this recipe it is a happy garnish for vegetables, but it is just as wonderful as a topping for grilled steak or a spread for a turkey and roasted-vegetable sandwich.

Serves 2

SALAD

Extra-virgin olive oil

1 head romaine lettuce, cut in half lengthwise, with root end intact

Kosher salt and freshly ground black pepper

1 cup grape or cherry tomatoes

Squeeze of fresh lemon juice

4 slices sourdough bread

1 ear fresh corn, husked

LEMON AIOLI

1 small clove garlic, smashed and coarsely chopped

1 egg yolk

1 teaspoon grated lemon zest (from about ½ lemon)

2 teaspoons fresh lemon juice

1 teaspoon Dijon mustard

Dash of Worcestershire sauce

Kosher salt and freshly ground black pepper

2 tablespoons extra-virgin olive oil

½ cup avocado oil

1. Heat a large skillet over high heat. Drizzle oil over the cut side of the romaine halves and sprinkle with salt and pepper. Place the romaine, cut side down, in the skillet. Add the tomatoes, drizzle a little oil over them, and sprinkle with salt and pepper. When the romaine begins to brown on its edges in a minute or two, transfer it to a serving platter, cut side up, and squeeze a little lemon juice over it. Transfer the tomatoes to the platter when one or two of them begin to burst.

2. Add the bread and ear of corn to the hot skillet, drizzle with a little oil, and sprinkle with salt and pepper. Toast the bread, about 3 minutes on each side. Remove the bread, reduce the heat to medium-low, and cover the skillet. Cook until the corn is tender, about 6 minutes. Transfer to a cutting board, and when the corn is cool enough to handle, cut the kernels from the cob.

3. To make the aioli, whisk the garlic, egg yolk, lemon zest, lemon juice, mustard, Worcestershire sauce, a pinch of salt, and several grinds of pepper together in a small bowl. Ever so slowly, while still whisking, dribble in the olive oil and avocado oil. After about a minute of dribbling in the oil, you can start to add it more quickly, while continuing to whisk. Alternatively, follow the same process in a food processor.

4. To finish assembling the salad, sprinkle the corn kernels over the romaine halves and tomatoes and drizzle with the aioli. Serve with the grilled bread.

Switch It Up!

MORE WAYS TO USE LEMON AIOLI

As a dip for raw veggies | In a Caesar dressing with romaine, Parmesan cheese, and croutons | As a dip for Spinach Balls (page 179) | With a chicken, tomato, and basil sandwich

Dinner in a Bowl

Buddha bowls or nourish bowls have become
popular ways to take a meal,
and our household has fully embraced this trend.
My philosophy is that adding a poached egg
to pretty much anything makes it dinner,
so we often do (see page 77 for how to poach).
It works with nearly any salad
or vegetarian dish we create. There are lots of
other ways to create delicious one-bowl
dinners, too. Following are some of my favorites.

TOFU AND SESAME SCRAMBLED EGGS WITH CUCUMBER AND CABBAGE

Most mornings are an early affair for me, no matter what the season. Coffee, no breakfast, and then by midmorning I'm ready to eat. When I'm trying to lower my carb intake, this meal is one that I turn to over and over again, and not only in the morning.

Sambal oelek can be found in the Asian section of most grocery stores. It's an Indonesian chili paste that can do pretty much anything. I mash it with avocado and serve it with black beans, swirl it into brothy soups, or toss it with some greens, a little lime juice, and some sesame oil.

Save the seeds from the cucumber to make cucumber lemon water, a refreshing drink you can enjoy after a workout or on the deck at the end of a warm day.

Serves 2

1 cucumber

Juice from a wedge of fresh lime

3 cups thinly sliced Napa cabbage, also known as Chinese or Savoy cabbage

Tamari

1 cup diced firm tofu

¼ cup coarsely chopped fresh cilantro

¼ cup thinly sliced scallions (about 1 scallion)

2 eggs

1 teaspoon sesame oil

2 tablespoons sambal oelek, for garnish

¼ cup coarsely ground unsalted peanuts, for garnish

1. Peel thin strips of the cucumber lengthwise with a vegetable peeler down to the seeds in the center, turning as needed. Divide the cucumber strips evenly between two bowls and squeeze some fresh lime juice over top.

2. Add the cabbage to the bowls, along with a dash of tamari. Top with the tofu, cilantro, and scallions.

3. Beat the eggs with a dash of tamari in a small bowl. Heat the oil in a small skillet over high heat, add the eggs, and stir quickly with a fork. As soon as the eggs are just cooked through, 1 to 2 minutes, remove from the skillet and divide between the bowls.

4. Garnish the bowls with sambal oelek and peanuts.

GARLIC AND GINGER PORK BOWLS WITH CUCUMBER, MINT, AND CILANTRO

The contrast between the heat from the chiles and ginger and the coolness of the mint and cucumber creates a wonderful, opposites-attract combination. This dish continues to be among my absolute favorites. Most of the time, I don't care about having the same thing more than once. Usually, creativity, fun, and experimentation is the name of the food game. However, this meal? Several nights in a row, no problem.

Serves 2

¾ cup jasmine rice

1½ cups water

Fat pinch of kosher salt

1 cup diced cucumber (about ½ cucumber)

2 tablespoons minced scallions

2 tablespoons fresh lime juice (from about 1 lime)

2 tablespoons fish sauce (nam pla) (for both the cucumbers and the pork)

½ cup lightly packed fresh cilantro

½ cup lightly packed fresh mint

1 tablespoon peanut oil

½ pound ground pork

1 tablespoon minced garlic (about 3 cloves)

1 tablespoon grated fresh ginger

1 teaspoon minced Thai chile

2 lime wedges, for garnish

Sriracha, for garnish

1. To make the rice, combine the rice, water, and salt in a medium saucepan. Bring to a boil, then reduce the heat, cover, and let simmer for 15 minutes, or until the rice is tender. Remove from the heat and set aside.

2. Combine the cucumber, scallions, lime juice, and 1 tablespoon fish sauce in a small bowl and mix well. Fold in the cilantro and mint.

3. Heat the oil in a small skillet over medium-high heat. Add the pork and stir with a wooden spoon for a minute or two to break up the meat. Add the garlic, ginger, and chile and cook for 2 to 3 minutes, until the meat is browned. Stir in the remaining 1 tablespoon of fish sauce.

4. Divide the cooked rice between two bowls. Top with the pork and the cucumber mixture. Serve with lime wedges and Sriracha.

SALMON, PEA SHOOT, AVOCADO, AND BROWN RICE WITH WASABI MAYONNAISE

I could happily have this ultimate meal-in-a-bowl every day for quite some time. The creamy salmon and the punch of wasabi balance amazingly well with the crunchy pea shoots and the nutty brown rice. Most tender greens work well in this dish; my favorites are mixed greens, spring mix, and spinach. Exceptionally fresh salmon is a must in this recipe, so purchase it from a local fishmonger whom you trust.

Serves 2

- 1 hot red Thai or other chile pepper, thinly sliced

  Kosher salt

- 2 tablespoons rice wine vinegar, plus a dash for seasoning the rice

- ¾ cup brown rice

- 2 cups lightly packed pea shoots

- 8 ounces very fresh salmon, skin removed, cut into ½-inch cubes

- 6 baby cucumbers, thinly sliced, or 1 cup diced cucumber

- 2 tablespoons fresh lime juice (from about 1 lime)

- 2 tablespoons tamari

- ½ avocado

- 2 tablespoons sesame seeds

WASABI MAYONNAISE

- 2 tablespoons mayonnaise

- 2 teaspoons wasabi powder

- 1 teaspoon fresh lime juice

- 1 teaspoon tamari

1. Toss the pepper slices with a pinch of salt in a small bowl and let sit for 10 minutes. Add 2 tablespoons vinegar, stir, and set aside.

2. To make the wasabi mayonnaise, combine the mayonnaise, wasabi powder, lime juice, and tamari in a small bowl and mix well.

3. Put the rice in a small pot with a pinch of salt and cover generously with water. Bring to a boil over high heat, then reduce the heat, and let simmer uncovered for 30 minutes. Drain the rice and transfer to a medium bowl. Add a dash of vinegar and a pinch of salt and mix gently. Let cool until the rice is lukewarm.

4. Divide the rice between two large bowls. Nestle the pea shoots next to the rice and drizzle 1 teaspoon of the pickled pepper juice (the vinegar that the chile pepper slices have been sitting in) on top.

5. Combine the salmon, cucumbers, lime juice, and tamari in a small bowl and mix gently. Divide evenly over the rice.

6. Scoop avocado pieces onto the pea shoots and top with the chile pepper slices, wasabi mayonnaise, and sesame seeds. Serve immediately.

PAN-SEARED EGGPLANT AND KISIR WITH WALNUT FIG YOGURT

Kisir is the lesser-known sibling of tabbouleh. It is a bulgur-based tomato salad, with cumin and chili flakes sprinkled in for a bit of pleasant depth. Pomegranate molasses can be found in the Middle Eastern section of most grocery stores and is well worth the search. See page 45 for ideas on how to use it in other dishes.

Serves 2

KISIR

- 1 tablespoon extra-virgin olive oil
- ½ cup minced onion (about 1 small onion)
  Kosher salt and freshly ground black pepper
- 2 tablespoons tomato paste
- ½ teaspoon minced garlic (about ½ clove)
- 1 teaspoon ground cumin
  Tiny pinch of red pepper flakes
- 1 cup diced tomatoes (canned or fresh)
- ¾ cup bulgur
- ½ cup water
- 1 teaspoon pomegranate molasses
- 1 teaspoon fresh lemon juice
- 2 tablespoons coarsely chopped mint
- 2 tablespoons coarsely chopped fresh flat-leaf parsley

WALNUT FIG YOGURT

- ½ cup Greek yogurt
- ⅓ cup coarsely chopped walnuts
- 1 dry fig, minced
- 1 teaspoon grated lemon zest (from about ½ lemon)
- 1 teaspoon fresh lemon juice
  Pinch of kosher salt

EGGPLANT

- 1 tablespoon extra-virgin olive oil, plus more as needed
- ½ eggplant, cut into ½-inch slices (about 8 ounces)
  Kosher salt and freshly ground black pepper

- 3 cups lightly packed arugula
- 2 tablespoons pomegranate seeds, for garnish

Recipe continues on next page

1. To make the kisir, heat the oil in a small saucepan over medium-high heat. Add the onions, season with a pinch of salt and several grinds of pepper, and sauté until the onions are soft and translucent, 7 to 10 minutes. Add the tomato paste, garlic, cumin, and red pepper flakes and stir well. Add the diced tomatoes, sprinkle with salt, and stir in the bulgur and water. Cover and set aside for 10 minutes to allow the bulgur to absorb the moisture. Then add the pomegranate molasses, lemon juice, mint, and parsley and mix gently.

2. To make the walnut fig yogurt, combine the yogurt, walnuts, fig, lemon zest, lemon juice, and salt in a small bowl and mix well.

3. To cook the eggplant, heat the oil in a medium skillet over medium-high heat. Add the eggplant, sprinkle with salt and pepper, and cook until the eggplant is browned on the outside and tender in the center, 4 to 5 minutes on each side, adding a little extra oil if it seems dry.

4. To serve, mound the arugula in two serving bowls. Top each one with kisir, eggplant, and a good dollop of the walnut fig yogurt. Garnish with pomegranate seeds.

Switch It Up!

MORE WAYS TO USE WALNUT FIG YOGURT

On caramelized carrots and parsnips | On toast | With seared greens | On pizza with olives and tomatoes | As a dip for apples

VIETNAMESE RICE NOODLE SALAD WITH CARROTS, RADISHES, AND BEAN SPROUTS

I have a mandolin in my kitchen, so julienning all these vegetables isn't an issue. However, you can achieve the same results using a vegetable peeler and taking off 2-inch strips of the carrot and radishes until only a nub is left. Keep everything super cold by putting each ingredient back into the fridge once the prep is finished.

Serves 2

RICE NOODLE SALAD

- 4 ounces thin rice noodles (¼ of a 1-pound package)
- 1 cup julienned carrots (about 1 carrot)
- 1 cup julienned daikon radish (about a 3-inch piece of daikon)
- 1 cup thinly sliced radishes (about 4 radishes)
- 2 cups lightly packed green leaf lettuce
- 1 cup bean sprouts
- ¼ cup fresh cilantro, for garnish
- ¼ cup fresh mint, for garnish
- ¼ cup coarsely chopped unsalted peanuts, for garnish

  Sriracha or other Asian-style hot sauce

DRESSING

- 2 tablespoons fish sauce (nam pla)
- 2 tablespoons fresh lime juice (from about 1 lime)
- 2 tablespoons rice wine vinegar
- 2 tablespoons sesame oil
- ¼ teaspoon sugar

1. Hydrate the noodles by soaking them in very hot water for 15 to 20 minutes, or by following the package instructions. Drain well.

2. To make the dressing, combine the fish sauce, lime juice, rice wine vinegar, sesame oil, and sugar in a small bowl and mix well.

3. Divide the noodles and vegetables between two dinner bowls, arranging them in little mounds. Drizzle the dressing over everything and then garnish with cilantro, mint, peanuts, and hot sauce.

SALT-CURED SALMON WITH BEETS, CUCUMBERS, SNAP PEAS, AND HORSERADISH DILL CREAM

This is one of those meals that is perfect for the heat of the summer but could easily be brunch or a winter dinner as well. It is a crowd-pleaser with a pretty fabulous "wow" factor, as in, "Wow! You made this yourself?!" The number of vegetables in this dish makes my heart happy on so many levels. Be sure to give the salmon enough time to cure.

Serves 2

SALMON BOWL

- 8 ounces fresh salmon
- 2 tablespoons kosher salt
- 2 teaspoons sugar
- 2 beets, trimmed
- ½ English cucumber, thinly sliced
- 1 cup snap peas
  Fresh dill sprigs, for garnish
- 2 slices rye bread

PICKLED SHALLOTS

- ⅓ cup rice wine vinegar
- 1 tablespoon apple cider vinegar
- 2 tablespoons water
- 1 tablespoon sugar
- 1½ teaspoons kosher salt
- 1 cup thinly sliced shallots (about 4 shallots)

HORSERADISH DILL CREAM

- ¼ cup crème fraîche
- 1 tablespoon prepared horseradish
- 2 teaspoons minced fresh dill
  Kosher salt and freshly ground black pepper

1. Set the salmon in a small, high-sided non-reactive pan and rub with the salt and sugar. Cover with plastic wrap and refrigerate for 24 hours.

2. Cover the beets with water in a small pot. Bring to a boil over high heat and boil for 20 to 30 minutes, until the beets are tender when pierced with a knife. Drain and set aside. When the beets are cool enough to handle, peel them and cut each one into eight wedges.

3. To make the pickled shallots, bring the rice wine vinegar, apple cider vinegar, water, sugar, and salt to a boil in a small saucepan. Turn off the heat, add the shallots, stir, and set aside to cool.

4. To make the horseradish dill cream, combine the crème fraîche, horseradish, dill, a pinch of salt, and a few grinds of pepper in a small bowl.

5. To assemble, slice the salmon very thinly. Set small mounds of the beets, cucumbers, and snap peas in two dinner bowls. Add the salmon, top with a little mound of the pickled shallots, and then drizzle the vegetables with the horseradish cream and garnish with the dill sprigs. Serve immediately, while the salmon is still cold, with rye bread.

Switch It Up!

MORE WAYS TO USE HORSERADISH DILL CREAM

With seared salmon | On potato pancakes | On toast with avocado, radishes, and microgreens

SOBA AND BROCCOLI WITH GINGER-GARLIC PEANUT SAUCE

This dish is so full of flavor that the fact that it's vegetarian can pass by unnoticed. In the absence of meat, a dish can lack that typically deep, agreeable umami quality, but the soba noodles, peanuts, and tamari deliver it here with aplomb.

Serves 2

SOBA AND BROCCOLI

Kosher salt

3 ounces soba noodles

1 large head broccoli, cut into florets (about 5 cups)

1 cup julienned carrots (about 1 carrot)

1 cup bean sprouts

¼ cup fresh cilantro, for garnish

¼ cup fresh mint, for garnish

¼ cup coarsely chopped unsalted peanuts, for garnish

Sriracha or other Asian-flavored hot sauce (optional)

GINGER-GARLIC PEANUT SAUCE

1 tablespoon peanut or canola oil

1 cup thinly sliced shallots (about 4 shallots)

1 Thai red chile, seeded and minced

1 tablespoon minced garlic (about 3 cloves)

1 tablespoon grated fresh ginger

⅓ cup coarsely chopped unsalted peanuts

1 tablespoon sugar

2 tablespoons fresh lime juice (from about 1 lime)

2 tablespoons tamari

1 tablespoon sesame oil

1–4 tablespoons water

1. Bring a medium pot of salted water to a boil over high heat. Add the noodles and cook for 4 minutes. Use a slotted spoon or sieve to transfer the noodles to a colander to drain and then divide them between two dinner bowls.

2. Add the broccoli to the boiling water and cook for 3 to 6 minutes, until it is tender but still bright green. Transfer the broccoli to the colander to drain.

3. To make the sauce, heat the peanut oil in a medium skillet over medium-high heat. Add the shallots and sauté until they become translucent, 7 to 10 minutes. Add the chile, garlic, and ginger and stir until fragrant, 30 seconds to 1 minute. Add the peanuts and the sugar and stir until the sugar has melted and begins to smell caramelized, 2 to 3 minutes. Add the lime juice, tamari, and sesame oil and enough water to thin the sauce so that it can be drizzled.

4. To assemble the dish, arrange the broccoli on top of the noodles and then nestle the carrots and bean sprouts next to the broccoli. Drizzle the sauce over everything and garnish with cilantro, mint, and peanuts. Top with a little Sriracha, if desired.

CHILI-RUBBED RIB-EYE STEAK WITH CHIMICHURRI AND SEARED GREEN BEANS, TOMATOES, AND SMASHED GARLIC

Chimichurri sauce normally has oregano as one of its primary ingredients, but that seasoning has always tasted harsh to me. So, while I greatly respect culinary traditions, I can't bring myself to follow this one. If you would prefer to replace some of the cilantro with oregano, you will surely satisfy the traditionalists.

Serves 2

- 1½ teaspoons chili powder
- 1½ teaspoons ground cumin
- Kosher salt
- 1 (1-pound) rib-eye steak, about ¾ inch thick
- 1 tablespoon extra-virgin olive oil
- 8 ounces fresh green beans
- 3 cloves garlic, smashed
- 1 tomato, cut into wedges

CHIMICHURRI SAUCE

- ¼ cup minced fresh cilantro
- ¼ cup minced scallions, green parts only (about 2 scallions; reserve the white parts for another recipe)
- 1 teaspoon minced jalapeño
- ½ teaspoon minced garlic (about ½ clove)
- Pinch of kosher salt
- 1 tablespoon extra-virgin olive oil
- 1½ teaspoons white wine vinegar

Recipe continues on next page

1. Combine the chili powder, cumin, and ½ teaspoon salt and mix well. Rub the spice mixture onto both sides of the steak to thoroughly coat it, and then let the steak sit on a platter for 10 minutes.

2. To make the chimichurri sauce, combine cilantro, scallions, jalapeño to taste, garlic, salt, oil, and vinegar in a small bowl. Mix well and set aside.

3. Heat the oil in a medium skillet over medium-high heat. Add the steak and the green beans and sprinkle the green beans with a pinch of salt. Sear the steak for 4 to 6 minutes, depending on how well done you would like it. (Note that any variation in the thickness of the steak will affect the cooking time.)

4. Flip the steak to the other side. Add the garlic cloves to the skillet, tossing them with the beans, and sauté for 2 minutes. Then add the tomatoes and sprinkle them with a tiny pinch of salt. When some of the beans are blistered and the tomatoes are cooked through, about 2 minutes, transfer them to two dinner bowls, dividing them evenly.

5. Continue searing the steak until an instant-read thermometer registers an internal temperature of 120°F (49°C) for medium rare, another 1 to 2 minutes. Transfer the steak to a cutting board and let it rest for 5 minutes. Then slice it thinly and arrange the slices on top of the beans. Top with the chimichurri sauce and serve.

Switch It Up!

MORE WAYS TO USE CHIMICHURRI

Mixed with yogurt on poached chicken | With seared lamb chops | On toast with sliced tomato and Monterey Jack cheese

CHAPTER 6

STOVETOP ONE-PAN WONDERS

Using only one pan or pot to create
a meal takes a bit of ingenuity,
but it saves gobs of time and energy
in the cleanup department, not to mention
all the space-saving benefits.
That said, there's no swapping efficiency
for quality in these recipes—they are still delish.
Whether on the stovetop or in the oven,
there are many options for
creating a meal with only one pan.

In the Skillet

There are a lot of good skillets out there,
but a cast-iron skillet is the
workhorse of the kitchen. It is oven safe and
therefore can double as both a
stovetop pan and a roasting pan.
When combined with a lid, a skillet's uses
grow exponentially. The lid
keeps things from splattering all over the place—
again, a real saver of time and energy
in cleanup. It also traps heat and
allows thicker and heavier items
a chance to cook through and catch up
with the heat on the exterior.

CHICKEN TOSTADA WITH LIME CREMA AND ANCHO CHILE SPREAD

This simple dish is crunchy, light, and bright. The sunny blend of tomatoes and cilantro is both charming and lively paired with the creamy lime crema and the zingy ancho chile spread, a perfect example of simple ingredients becoming more than their parts.

Try it with some pickled jalapeños (page 95) instead of the ancho chile spread, or top it with some queso fresco.

Serves 2

ANCHO CHILE SPREAD

- 3 dried ancho chiles, seeds removed
- 4 cloves garlic, unpeeled
- ½ teaspoon dried Mexican oregano
- Pinch of ground cumin
- Pinch of kosher salt

TOSTADAS

- ½ cup peanut or canola oil
- 4 small corn tortillas
- Kosher salt
- 2 teaspoons extra-virgin olive oil
- 2 cloves garlic, smashed
- 1 cup sliced onion (about 1 medium onion)
- 8 ounces boneless chicken thighs, thinly sliced (about 2 thighs)
- Freshly ground black pepper
- 6 cherry tomatoes, sliced in half
- ½ avocado, sliced
- Chopped fresh cilantro

LIME CREMA

- ¼ cup sour cream
- ¼ cup low-fat or whole-milk plain yogurt
- 1 teaspoon grated lime zest (from about ½ lime)
- 1 teaspoon fresh lime juice
- Pinch of kosher salt

1. To make the ancho chile spread, heat a small skillet over medium heat. Add the chiles, pressing them down flat with a spatula. When they begin to crackle, turn and do the same on the other side. Transfer the chiles to a small bowl of hot water and let sit for 30 minutes, making sure the water covers them. Drain, reserving 3 tablespoons of the liquid.

2. Meanwhile, add the garlic to the same skillet you used for the chiles. Roast until the cloves are soft and brown on the outside, 5 to 7 minutes. Remove from the pan, let cool, and peel.

3. Mince the garlic, chiles, oregano, cumin, and salt to a smooth paste or process the ingredients in a food processor. Add some of the reserved chile soaking water to thin the mixture, if needed.

4. To make the tostadas, lay a paper towel on a plate. Heat the peanut oil in a medium skillet over medium-high heat. When the oil is hot, fry the tortillas one at a time, flipping them as each side gets brown, about 30 seconds per side. Transfer to the towel-lined plate and sprinkle a tiny pinch of salt over each one. Carefully drain the peanut oil from the skillet, and wipe it out with a paper towel.

5. Heat the olive oil in the same skillet over medium-high heat. Add the garlic, onions, and chicken and sprinkle with salt and pepper. Sauté until the onions are translucent and the chicken is cooked through, 7 to 10 minutes.

6. To make the crema, whisk the sour cream, yogurt, lime zest, lime juice, and salt together in a small bowl.

7. Top the tostadas with the chicken, halved tomatoes, sliced avocado, and cilantro. Add a dollop of lime crema and ancho chile spread and serve immediately.

HERBED REDFISH WITH LEMON AND LIME

While this is a great skillet recipe, it is also perfectly suited to outdoor cooking and benefits from the smoky flavor that only grilling can impart. If redfish isn't available, any small whole fish will do well in this versatile dish. It also bears mentioning that using the whole fish need not be intimidating. The cooking process is so simple and the results are so wonderful, you might never go back!

Serves 2

1½ pounds whole redfish, either one large or two small, scales and innards removed

2 tablespoons extra-virgin olive oil

Kosher salt and freshly ground black pepper

Several sprigs of fresh basil

Several sprigs of fresh cilantro

Several stalks of fresh chives

1 lemon, thinly sliced, seeds removed

1 lime, thinly sliced, seeds removed

1. Make two parallel slices down the middle of each side of the fish. Rub all over with the oil and sprinkle with salt and pepper. Stuff the fish with the basil, cilantro, and chives and a few slices of lemon and lime, reserving a few of the fresh herbs and citrus slices for garnishes.

2. Heat a skillet over medium-high heat. Carefully lay the fish in the skillet and sear for about 10 minutes on each side, until an instant-read thermometer registers an internal temperature of 140°F (60°C).

3. Transfer to a platter and garnish with the reserved fresh herbs and lemon and lime slices. To serve, use two flat spoons to gently lift the fish fillets away from the bones.

ROASTED CAULIFLOWER, FREGULA, BABY KALE, AND CODDLED EGGS

Fregula, a pasta hailing from Sardinia, is much like Israeli couscous. It's pretty and fun, and in Sardinia it is commonly simmered in a tomato sauce with clams. If you can't find it, though, you can substitute orzo or Israeli couscous, which are also pasta shapes. To incorporate a grain instead, try farro or spelt.

The cauliflower takes a good hour in the oven, but the caramelized, crispy exterior is worth it. To make the best use of energy and space, I usually roast some other veggies at the same time to add to a salad or dinner on another night.

Serves 2

   6 large cauliflower florets (about ½ head cauliflower)

   2 teaspoons extra-virgin olive oil

     Kosher salt

   ½ cup fregula, orzo, or Israeli couscous (or 1½ cups cooked fregula)

   1 teaspoon coconut oil

   ½ cup diced onion (about 1 small onion)

   1 red bell pepper, cut into 1-inch pieces

   1 teaspoon minced garlic (about 1 clove)

   ½ teaspoon garam masala

   1 fresh tomato, cut into wedges, or 1 cup whole canned tomatoes with juice

 2–4 eggs (depending on how hungry you are)

   3 cups lightly packed baby kale and beet greens

1. Preheat the oven to 450°F (230°C).

2. Arrange the cauliflower in a small ovenproof skillet or pie plate. Drizzle with the oil and sprinkle with a pinch of salt. Roast for 1 hour, or until the edges are browned and the centers are tender.

3. Meanwhile, bring a small pot of salted water to a boil. Add the fregula and cook according to the package instructions until al dente, then drain.

4. Heat the coconut oil in a small skillet over medium-high heat. Add the onions, sprinkle with salt, and sauté for 7 to 10 minutes, until translucent. Add the bell pepper, garlic, and garam masala and sauté for another 5 minutes. Add the tomatoes and fregula and bring to a simmer, then break the eggs into the skillet, sprinkle with salt, cover, and cook for 2 to 4 minutes, depending on how well cooked you prefer your eggs.

5. Remove the fregula and eggs from the heat. Arrange the roasted cauliflower and the baby kale and beet greens on top of the fregula and serve.

TURKEY WITH PRESERVED LEMON AND DILL GREMOLATA, ASPARAGUS, AND CAULIFLOWER

This sort of meal, where everything is tidily made in one pan, makes such sense for a small kitchen—or any kitchen, really. Who wants to wash four pans if you could wash just one?

Preserved lemons are a gem for the pantry. Once you have them, you'll never go back. They are very salty, so a little bit goes a long way. You don't need a lot to make a meal sparkle.

Serves 2

- 2 tablespoons extra-virgin olive oil
- 2 turkey cutlets (about 4 ounces each)
- ½ head cauliflower, cut into florets (about 3 cups)
- Kosher salt and freshly ground black pepper
- 1 bunch asparagus

LEMON AND DILL GREMOLATA

- 2 tablespoons minced fresh dill
- 2 tablespoons minced preserved lemons (see following page)
- Freshly ground black pepper

1. Heat 1 tablespoon of the oil in a medium skillet over medium-high heat. Add the turkey and cauliflower and sprinkle with salt and pepper. Sear the turkey for 2 to 3 minutes on each side, until just cooked through, and then transfer the cutlets to a platter, leaving the cauliflower in the skillet to keep cooking.

2. Add the asparagus to the skillet, drizzle with the remaining 1 tablespoon oil, and sprinkle with salt and pepper. Cook for 4 to 5 minutes, until the asparagus is crisp-tender and bright green. Transfer the asparagus to the platter with the turkey, still leaving the cauliflower in the skillet. Cover the skillet and continue to cook until the cauliflower is tender in the middle and the edges are browned, another 3 to 4 minutes. Transfer the cauliflower to the platter.

3. To make the gremolata, combine the dill, preserved lemon, and a few grinds of pepper in a small bowl and mix well.

4. Scatter the gremolata over the turkey and vegetables and serve.

Switch It Up!
MORE WAYS TO USE LEMON AND DILL GREMOLATA
With heavy cream over pasta and fresh peas | Dotted over grilled bell peppers and zucchini | Spread on toast with cured salmon and sliced beets

Preserved Lemons

If preserved lemons are hard to find, no worries—they are easy
to make. Cut one lemon into wedges and combine in a jar with
3 tablespoons kosher salt and 3 tablespoons extra-virgin olive oil.
Shake well. Let marinate for at least 2 weeks, shaking every day.
The lemons will keep for up to 3 months.

CREAMY CHICKEN WITH KALE PESTO, BABY POTATOES, AND ARUGULA

This pesto is milder than the fragrant basil variety, with a slightly bitter note. It's a star in our house, where we use it in soups, pastas, and sandwiches and on pizzas—any way you might use a traditional pesto. If you have someone with a pine nut allergy, sunflower seeds are an excellent substitute.

Serves 2

8 ounces baby red potatoes (about 12 potatoes)

Kosher salt

1 tablespoon extra-virgin olive oil, plus a drizzle for the arugula

1 small onion, cut into 1-inch pieces (about ½ cup)

Freshly ground black pepper

8 ounces boneless chicken thighs, cut into 1-inch cubes (about 2 thighs)

¼ cup heavy cream

2 cups lightly packed arugula

Squeeze of fresh lemon juice

Grated Parmesan cheese, for garnish

KALE PESTO

2 ounces kale, stems removed (about 2 cups lightly packed)

1 tablespoon pine nuts

½ clove garlic

2 tablespoons grated Parmesan cheese

1 tablespoon extra-virgin olive oil

Kosher salt and freshly ground black pepper

1. Put the potatoes in a medium saucepan, add enough water to cover them, and salt it well. Bring to a boil over high heat and boil for 15 minutes, or until the potatoes are tender when pierced with a knife. Drain and set aside.

2. Meanwhile, to make the kale pesto, finely mince the kale, pine nuts, and garlic and combine in a small bowl with the Parmesan, oil, a pinch of salt, and several grinds of pepper. Alternatively, pulse in a small food processor.

3. Heat the oil in a medium skillet over medium-high heat. Add the onions and sprinkle with salt and pepper. Sauté for 7 minutes, or until the onions begin to soften. Then add the chicken thighs and a little more salt and pepper. Cook for 5 minutes. When the chicken is nearly done, add the heavy cream and the pesto and stir well.

4. Arrange the arugula on two plates, drizzle with olive oil and a squeeze of lemon juice, and sprinkle with salt and pepper. Top with the chicken thighs and nestle the potatoes alongside them. Garnish with Parmesan.

EGGPLANT AND TOMATO WITH CUCUMBER LEMON SALAD AND LABNEH

Silky eggplant, acidic tomatoes, cool cucumber and lemon, nutty brown rice, and creamy labneh—the interplay of flavors and textures in this dish is irresistible, and definitely inspired by Middle Eastern cuisine. Like many recipes in this book, this one needs no meat to be satisfying. I prefer brown rice here, but white rice is perfectly acceptable too.

Labneh, a creamy white yogurt with the excess moisture strained from it, is ubiquitous in Middle Eastern cooking, and it's easy to see why—it's quite wonderful.

Serves 2

1 cup low-fat or whole-milk plain yogurt

¾ cup brown rice

3 tablespoons extra-virgin olive oil, plus a drizzle for serving

½ eggplant, cut into 1-inch cubes (about 4 cups)

1 small onion, cut into 1-inch pieces (about ½ cup)

Kosher salt and freshly ground black pepper

1 teaspoon ground cardamom

1 teaspoon ground cumin

1 tomato, cut into 1-inch cubes (about 1 cup)

CUCUMBER LEMON SALAD

½ cup finely diced cucumber

½ teaspoon minced garlic (about ½ clove)

Pinch of kosher salt

½ teaspoon fresh lemon juice

Freshly ground black pepper

Rice, Faster

Steaming is the most common method of cooking rice to perfection. With most white rices, steaming takes about 20 minutes. With brown rice, it takes 45 minutes to an hour. But boiling the rice and then draining it, as directed in this recipe, shortens the cooking time considerably. A lid is not required while boiling.

1. To make the labneh, tie the yogurt up in a piece of cheesecloth and poke the handle of a wooden spoon through the knot. Rest the wooden spoon over a deep bowl and let the yogurt hang for at least 8 hours or overnight in the refrigerator.

2. Put the rice in a small pot with a pinch of salt and cover generously with water. Bring to a boil over high heat, then reduce the heat and let simmer for 30 minutes. Drain.

3. Heat the oil in a medium skillet over medium-high heat. Add the eggplant and onion and sprinkle with a pinch of salt and several grinds of pepper. Cook for 7 to 10 minutes, until the eggplant and onion become slightly tender. Sprinkle with the cardamom and cumin, add the tomato, and stir. Cook for another 4 to 5 minutes, until the tomatoes are warmed through.

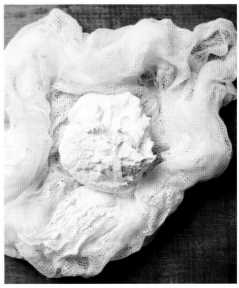

Recipe continues on next page

4. To make the cucumber salad, mix the cucumber, garlic, and salt in a small bowl and let sit for at least 15 minutes. Drain any liquid and then stir in the lemon juice and several grinds of pepper.

5. When you're ready to serve, form the labneh into six small rounds with your hands. Arrange the rice in two bowls and top with the eggplant mixture, the cucumber salad, and the labneh. Drizzle a little olive oil over the labneh.

Switch It Up!

MORE WAYS TO USE LABNEH

While labneh can traditionally be rolled into balls and paired with extra-virgin olive oil, it's also wonderful as a spread, dip, or garnish:

With raw carrots and cucumbers as a snack | With chili and garlic oil over cauliflower | With chutney over broccoli and chicken | With roasted veggies, cilantro, and toasted almonds

HONEY, CHILI, AND LIME CHICKEN WITH APPLES, SHALLOTS, AND DELICATA SQUASH

Pure fall, this dish is one I think of after an afternoon of picking apples or cleaning up in the garden. The recipe came to me as I was pulling the remnants of the squash vines from a side bed where they roam free. There, under cover, were a couple of delicata squash that I had missed. The resulting dish is warm, comforting, and cozy. Just the thing on a chilly fall night.

Serves 2

- 2 tablespoons coarsely chopped pecans

  Kosher salt

- 2 tablespoons extra-virgin olive oil

- 2 boneless chicken thighs (about 4 ounces each)

- 3 shallots, cut into ½-inch wedges

- 1 apple, peeled, cored, and cut into ½-inch cubes

- 2 teaspoons chili powder

  Drizzle of honey (about 1 teaspoon)

- 1 delicata squash, cut into 1-inch cubes (about 2 cups)

  Grated lime zest

- 1 teaspoon fresh lime juice

1. Heat a medium skillet over medium-high heat. Add the pecans and a pinch of salt and cook, stirring fairly continuously, until they begin to smell nutty and are lightly toasted, 2 to 3 minutes. Transfer the pecans to a small bowl.

2. Heat 1 tablespoon of the olive oil in the same skillet over medium-high heat. Add the chicken, shallots, apple, chili powder, and a pinch of salt. Cook the chicken for 5 to 8 minutes on each side, until cooked through, while stirring up the shallots and apple occasionally. Transfer the shallots and apples to a platter when they are brown on the edges and tender in the center. Continue to cook the chicken, if needed. When the chicken is done, add it to the platter and drizzle it all with a little honey.

3. Return the skillet to medium-high heat. Add the remaining 1 tablespoon olive oil, the squash, and a pinch of salt. Sear the squash for 2 to 4 minutes, until the edges begin to brown. Then reduce the heat to medium-low, cover, and cook, stirring occasionally, for 10 to 15 minutes, until the squash is tender on the inside and nicely browned on the outside.

4. Transfer the squash to the platter with the chicken, shallots, and apples. Sprinkle the lime zest over the chicken to taste, and squeeze lime juice over everything. Scatter the toasted pecans on top and serve.

PANCETTA, TOMATO, AND PARMESAN GEMELLI

Salty pancetta, fresh tomatoes, and tangy Parmesan are a classic combination I can't walk away from. Sometimes, familiar comfort food is exactly what's needed. No experimentation, nothing extraordinary... except the perfect blend of flavors that exactly hit the spot.

Serves 2

2 ounces pancetta, diced

1 cup sliced onion (about 1 medium onion)

2 cups diced fresh tomatoes (about 2 tomatoes)

2 tablespoons sliced garlic (about 2 cloves)

6 ounces gemelli pasta

2¼ cups chicken broth

2 tablespoons extra-virgin olive oil

½ teaspoon kosher salt

Freshly ground black pepper

¼ cup grated Parmesan cheese

1. Heat a large skillet over medium-high heat. Add the pancetta and fry for 3 to 4 minutes, until the fat begins to render. Add the onion and sauté for 3 to 4 minutes, until it begins to soften, and then add the tomatoes, garlic, gemelli, chicken broth, oil, salt, and several grinds of pepper. Bring to a boil, then reduce the heat and let simmer for 10 to 12 minutes, stirring often, until the pasta is al dente.

2. Transfer to a platter, sprinkle with Parmesan, and serve.

One-Pan Pasta

Most of us have been taught that pasta is cooked separately and then added to the sauce, but the cooking can all be done in one pan—and with great results. At first it doesn't seem like it will work, but it will. Believe. In the end, the pasta is coated in a silky sauce created by the starchy binder that the pasta releases into the cooking liquid. Many pasta sauce recipes call for a ladle of the pasta cooking water for just this reason.

I use this technique in two recipes in this book: Pancetta, Tomato, and Parmesan Gemelli (148) and Preserved Lemon, Ricotta, and Pea Orecchiette (151). If you experiment with your own one-pan pasta recipes, here a few tips for success.

— If any ingredient will benefit from being sautéed, such as pancetta, do that first.

— Monitor closely! Once everything is in the pan, don't walk away or start talking on the phone. Constant stirring isn't required, but regular and consistent stirring is.

— Once the liquid in the pan comes to a boil, reduce the heat so that everything stays at a nice little simmer.

— Add salt to the cooking liquid. As the pasta absorbs the liquid, the salt will help bump up the flavors.

— If you are using an ingredient that takes very little time to cook, such as shrimp, add it at the very end so you can remove the pan from the heat as soon as it is done.

— Dry, store-bought noodles work the best—this is *not* a technique for fresh pasta, which will simply fall apart and create a gloppy mess.

— Gluten-free noodles will not yield the silky sauce that is the usual beautiful result of this method of cooking. However, they will still create a lovely one-pot meal.

PRESERVED LEMON, RICOTTA, AND PEA ORECCHIETTE

Fresh peas and preserved lemon give this pasta dish a decidedly bright spring taste—light, refreshing, and a bit creamy all at the same time. If you can't find preserved lemons, make your own (see page 140), or use instead 2 more tablespoons of lemon juice plus ½ teaspoon of kosher salt. The dish won't be quite as tangy, but it will still be delicious.

Serves 2

- 1 tablespoon extra-virgin olive oil
- 1 cup sliced onion (about 1 medium onion)
- Freshly ground black pepper
- ¼ cup minced preserved lemons
- 2 tablespoons minced garlic (about 6 cloves)
- 2 cups chicken broth
- 4 ounces orecchiette (about 1½ cups)
- 6 ounces fresh or frozen peas (about 1½ cups)
- ¾ cup ricotta cheese
- 2 teaspoons grated lemon zest (from about 1 lemon)
- 3 tablespoons fresh lemon juice (from about 1 lemon)
- 2 tablespoons grated Parmesan cheese

1. Heat the oil in a medium skillet over medium-high heat. Add the onions, season with several grinds of black pepper, and sauté for 5 to 6 minutes, until they begin to soften. Add the preserved lemons and garlic and sauté for 30 seconds to 1 minute, until the garlic becomes fragrant, and then add the broth and orecchiette. Bring to a boil, then reduce heat and let simmer for 10 to 12 minutes, stirring often, until the pasta is al dente.

2. Add the peas, ricotta, lemon zest, and lemon juice and heat until the peas are fully cooked but still bright green, 2 to 3 minutes. Add a little water if the sauce begins to stick to the skillet.

3. Transfer to a platter, sprinkle with Parmesan, and serve.

ROASTED TOMATOES, COCONUT, CABBAGE, AND SHIITAKES OVER BASMATI RICE

These ingredients might seem like an odd combination, but this dish exceeds the sum of its parts. The tangy seared tomatoes, the sweet coconut, and the umami of the shiitakes become simply divine over the blank canvas of basmati rice.

Serves 2

- ¾ cup basmati rice
- 1½ cups water
- Kosher salt
- 2 tablespoons coconut oil
- 2 cups cherry tomatoes
- 1 cup canned coconut milk
- ½ cup diced onion (about 1 small onion)
- 1½ teaspoons minced garlic (about 1 large clove)
- 1½ teaspoons grated fresh ginger
- 3 cups thinly sliced green cabbage
- 3 ounces shiitake mushrooms, stemmed and sliced (about 1½ cups)
- 1 teaspoon fresh lime juice
- 1 tablespoon tamari
- 2 tablespoons coarsely chopped fresh cilantro, for garnish
- 2 tablespoons thinly sliced scallion, for garnish

1. Combine the rice, water, and a fat pinch of salt in a medium saucepan. Bring to a boil, then reduce heat, cover, and let simmer for 15 minutes, or until the rice is tender. Remove from the heat and set aside.

2. Heat 1 tablespoon of the coconut oil in a medium skillet over medium-high heat. Add the tomatoes, sprinkle with salt, cover partially, and cook for about 5 minutes, until the tomatoes are browned but not scorched. Add the coconut milk, bring to a simmer, and transfer to a small bowl.

3. Return the skillet to the heat and add the remaining 1 tablespoon coconut oil. Add the onion, garlic, and ginger and stir-fry until the onion begins to soften, about 4 minutes. Add the cabbage and shiitake mushrooms and stir-fry for another 4 minutes.

4. Return the tomatoes and coconut milk to the skillet with the cabbage and shiitakes. Add the lime juice and tamari and stir well. Serve immediately over the rice, garnished with cilantro and scallions.

MUSTARDY BALSAMIC-Y PORK
WITH CABBAGE AND POTATOES

When I was testing these recipes, my daughter and her longtime boyfriend, Tyler, were staying at the house—and thank goodness, because the table was burgeoning with food and we needed help eating it all. At the end of a rather longish day, my creativity began to wane and I asked them what I should do with the pork tenderloin. Tyler suggested, "What about something mustardy and balsamic-y?" We loved it, so here it is.

Brussels sprouts work nicely in place of the cabbage in this recipe. Cut them in half before adding them to the skillet.

Serves 2

8 baby red potatoes

   Kosher salt

2 teaspoons salted butter

   Freshly ground black pepper

1 tablespoon Dijon mustard

1 tablespoon whole-grain mustard

12 ounces pork tenderloin (about half of a tenderloin)

1 tablespoon extra-virgin olive oil

1 head baby green cabbage (or ¼ large head), cored and cut into ¾-inch wedges

1 teaspoon paprika

3 tablespoons high-quality balsamic vinegar

1. Put the potatoes in a medium stockpot, add enough water to cover them, and salt it well. Bring to a boil over high heat. Boil for 15 to 20 minutes, until they are tender when pierced with a fork. Drain the potatoes, transfer to a medium bowl, and gently stir in the butter, a pinch of salt, and several grinds of pepper.

2. Combine the Dijon and whole-grain mustards in a small bowl and rub the pork with the mixture. Heat the oil in a medium skillet over medium heat. Add the pork and cabbage and sprinkle with salt, pepper, and the paprika. Sear for 15 to 20 minutes, turning to caramelize the pork and cabbage on all sides, until an instant-read thermometer registers an internal temperature of 145°F (63°C) for the pork. Transfer the pork to a cutting board and let it rest for 5 minutes.

3. Return the skillet to the heat and add the balsamic vinegar, scraping up any browned bits from the bottom of the pan. The vinegar will quickly come to a boil. Swirl it around in the skillet quickly and transfer to a small ramekin.

4. To serve, thinly slice the pork before transferring it to a platter with the cabbage and the potatoes. Drizzle with the balsamic sauce.

JERK PORK TENDERLOIN WITH SEARED PUMPKIN AND MANGO MINT SALAD

For several years I cooked in the Caribbean, where I fell in love with pumpkin as a vegetable rather than something used exclusively in desserts or baked goods. All of the flavors in this dish remind me of my time on those verdant islands. Down there, everything got grilled—pumpkin, yams, pineapple, everything. And why not? This recipe calls for searing the pumpkin, but if you have a grill, then please be my guest. The pork takes well to the (not too spicy) jerk flavors.

Use sugar or pie pumpkins, not the ones you get for Halloween jack-o'-lanterns, which, though they make wonderfully ghoulish decorations, aren't very flavorful. Other winter squash will work well as substitutes.

Serves 2

MANGO MINT SALAD

- 1 mango, peeled and cut into long strips
- 1 tablespoon coarsely chopped fresh mint
- 1 tablespoon coarsely chopped fresh cilantro
- 1 teaspoon fresh lime juice
- Pinch of kosher salt
- Pinch of sugar

PORK AND PUMPKIN

- 12 ounces pork tenderloin (about half of a tenderloin)
- 1½ teaspoons jerk seasoning (one that's not too spicy)
- Kosher salt
- 1 tablespoon extra-virgin olive oil, plus a drizzle for the romaine
- 8 (3-inch) slices pumpkin, peeled and seeded
- 1 head baby red romaine lettuce
- Squeeze of lime juice
- Freshly ground black pepper

1. To make the mango salad, combine the mango, mint, cilantro, lime juice, salt, and sugar in a small bowl. Mix well and set aside.

2. Rub the pork with the jerk seasoning and a pinch of salt. Heat the oil in a medium skillet over medium heat. Add the pork and pumpkin and sprinkle the pumpkin with salt. Sear for 15 to 20 minutes, turning to caramelize the pork and pumpkin on all sides, until the pumpkin is tender and an instant-read thermometer registers an internal temperature of 145°F (63°C) for the pork. (Remove the pumpkin from the skillet before the pork if it's done earlier.) Transfer the pork to a cutting board and let it rest for 5 minutes.

3. Arrange the romaine leaves in a bowl or on a platter. Drizzle with oil and a squeeze of lime juice, and sprinkle with salt and pepper.

4. Thinly slice the pork, and drizzle any juices that collect on the cutting board over the lettuce leaves. Arrange the mango salad, pork slices, and pumpkin on the lettuce leaves and serve.

BRINED PORK CHOPS WITH GINGER AND LIME JULIENNED VEGETABLES

In the summertime, I can walk out to the garden and pick or pull all of the veggies used in this recipe. Sometimes, I might switch things up, reaching for tomatoes, scallions, zucchini, and orange pepper. In the wintertime, I might choose carrots, parsnips, fennel, and red onion. Ultimately, you can use any combination that gives you 4 cups of julienned veggies. If you don't have a mandolin for slicing them, a vegetable peeler works fine.

This is a generous recipe, since the pork chops are big and the veggies are plentiful. You could easily serve three or four people if folks were to share a chop. We usually end up with leftovers that serve us another night in a soup made with chicken broth and udon noodles, which suits us just fine. The chops can also be grilled instead of seared if you prefer to cook outdoors.

Serves 2

BRINED PORK CHOPS

- 2 cups hot water
- 3 tablespoons maple syrup
- 2 tablespoons kosher salt
- 2 cloves garlic, smashed
- 1 (1-inch) piece fresh ginger, thinly sliced
- 2 pork chops, 1½ inches thick (about 12 ounces each)
- 1 tablespoon peanut or canola oil

JASMINE RICE

- ¾ cup jasmine rice
- 1½ cups water
-    Fat pinch of kosher salt

GINGER AND LIME JULIENNED VEGETABLES

- 1 tablespoon extra-virgin olive oil
- 1 cup julienned carrots (about 1 carrot)
-    Kosher salt and freshly ground black pepper
- ½ cup julienned red bell pepper (about ½ pepper)
- 1 tablespoon julienned fresh ginger
- 1½ cups julienned snow peas (about 4 ounces)
- 1 cup julienned zucchini (about 1 zucchini)
- 1 teaspoon fresh lime juice

1. To make the brine, combine the water, maple syrup, salt, garlic, and ginger in a large bowl and stir. When the salt has dissolved and the water has cooled, submerge the pork chops in the brine. Make sure the pork chops are fully submerged. Cover the bowl and let the pork chops brine in the refrigerator for at least 8 hours or overnight.

2. Remove the pork chops from the brine and pat dry. Make sure they are dry or else they will splatter vigorously when you place them in the hot skillet.

3. To make the rice, combine the rice, water, and salt in a medium saucepan. Bring to a boil, then reduce the heat, cover, and let simmer for 15 minutes, or until the rice is tender. Remove from the heat and set aside, covered.

4. Meanwhile, heat a large skillet over medium-high heat. Add the peanut oil. Carefully place the pork chops in the skillet and partially cover with a lid to reduce splattering. Cook on each side about 10 minutes (reduce the heat to medium-low when searing the second side) or until an instant-read thermometer registers an internal temperature of 145°F (63°C). Set the chops aside on a platter to rest for 5 minutes.

5. Return the skillet to medium-high heat. Add the olive oil and then the carrots, sprinkle with a tiny bit of salt and pepper, and cook for 1 minute. Add the bell pepper and ginger, sprinkle with salt and pepper, and cook for another minute. Then add the snow peas and zucchini, sprinkle with salt and pepper, and cook for a final minute, or until the vegetables are all heated through. Stir in the lime juice and transfer to a platter.

6. Arrange the pork chops on top of the vegetables and serve with jasmine rice.

HONEY-ROASTED GRAPES WITH TURKEY AND TRICOLOR QUINOA AND RED CABBAGE

This is one of those dishes where all of the ingredients seem a bit mundane, but when combined, they create something very special. The honey-roasted grapes are my favorite; I like them so much, in fact, that sometimes I'll just roast some grapes that have lingered in the fridge and have them with yogurt on seedy toast. Here they burst with a juicy tang and a gentle sweetness that makes good friends with the quinoa and cabbage.

Serves 2

¾ cup tricolor quinoa

1½ cups plus 2 tablespoons water

Kosher salt

2 tablespoons extra-virgin olive oil

2 turkey cutlets, about ¼ inch thick (about 4 ounces each)

Freshly ground black pepper

2 cups red grapes

2 tablespoons white balsamic vinegar

2 tablespoons honey

2 cups thinly sliced red cabbage

1. Combine the quinoa, 1½ cups of the water, and a pinch of salt in a medium saucepan. Bring to a boil over high heat, then remove from the heat, cover, and let rest while you cook the turkey.

2. Heat 1 tablespoon of the oil in a medium skillet over medium-high heat. Carefully lay the turkey cutlets in the skillet and sprinkle with salt and pepper. Sear the turkey for 2 to 3 minutes on each side, and then transfer to a platter.

3. Add the grapes to the skillet and sear for 4 minutes, or until the skins begin to brown. Add the vinegar, the honey, and the remaining 2 tablespoons water. Reduce the heat to medium, cover, and let simmer for 10 minutes, or until the grapes begin to split and get a little mushy. Remove the lid and cook to reduce the sauce to a syrup, stirring occasionally, about 3 minutes. Use a spatula to scrape the sauce from the skillet into a small bowl; set aside.

4. Return the skillet to the heat and add the remaining 1 tablespoon oil and the cabbage. Sprinkle with salt and pepper. Cook for 5 minutes, or until the cabbage begins to wilt. Transfer the cabbage to a platter, top with the turkey, quinoa, and sauce, and serve.

SALMON WITH POTATO CAKES, SCALLION YOGURT, AND KALE

The lime and thyme add nice flavor to the otherwise traditional potato pancakes. Scallion yogurt is a delicious topping and is even better when made the day before and chilled overnight in the fridge.

Salmon is the creamiest of fish when it's not overcooked. To achieve that melt-in-your-mouth quality, remove it from the heat before the center has cooked all the way through. The residual heat will continue to cook the fish as it rests. I actually prefer my salmon done "medium," with a bit of a color difference in the center, so I'm careful to take it off the heat on the early side.

Serves 2

- 12 ounces salmon, cut into 2 equal pieces
- 2 tablespoons fresh lime juice (from about 1 lime)

  Kosher salt and freshly ground black pepper
- 12 ounces potatoes (about 5 medium potatoes)
- 1 large egg
- 1 teaspoon grated lime zest (from about ½ lime)
- 1 teaspoon fresh lime juice
- ½ teaspoon minced fresh thyme
- 1 tablespoon plus 1 teaspoon extra-virgin olive oil
- 3 cups lightly packed kale
- ½ cup diced fresh tomato (about ½ tomato)

SCALLION YOGURT

- ¼ cup plain Greek yogurt
- 2 tablespoons minced scallions, green parts only (reserve the white parts for another recipe)
- ½ teaspoon minced garlic (about ½ clove)
- 1 teaspoon grated lime zest (about ½ lime)
- 1 teaspoon fresh lime juice

  Pinch of kosher salt

1. Place the salmon on a platter and rub with the lime juice, a pinch of salt, and several grinds of pepper. Set aside.

2. Place a strainer in the sink or over a bowl. Peel the potatoes and grate them into the strainer. Add a pinch of salt and toss with your hands to combine. Press down on the potatoes to squeeze out any excess water. Transfer the potatoes to a medium bowl, add the egg, lime zest, lime juice, and thyme, and mix well.

3. Heat a medium skillet over medium-low heat and add 1 tablespoon of the oil. Divide the potato mixture into four rounds and press them flat in the skillet. Cook for 4 to 5 minutes on each side, until the potato cakes are nicely browned and cooked through. Transfer to two plates or a platter.

4. Heat the remaining 1 teaspoon oil in a small skillet over medium-high heat. Carefully place the salmon in the skillet and sear for 3 to 4 minutes on each side, until the center is still slightly darker pink and the outside has a nice crust. Remove from the heat and let rest.

5. Heat the medium skillet (the same one you used for the potato cakes) over medium-high heat. Add the kale and tomato and sprinkle with salt and pepper. Cook, turning with tongs, for 3 to 4 minutes, until the kale has wilted but is still bright green. Transfer to the plates or platter with the potato cakes.

6. Combine the yogurt, scallions, garlic, lime zest, lime juice, and salt in a small bowl and mix well, or pulse in a small food processor.

7. To serve, arrange the salmon on top of the kale and potato pancakes. Garnish with the scallion yogurt.

Switch It Up!

MORE WAYS TO USE SCALLION YOGURT

Swirled into tomato soup | As a salad dressing with radishes, peas, and walnuts | Drizzled over roasted cauliflower or steamed broccoli

CHICKEN, QUINOA, AND ARUGULA WITH BALSAMIC CHERRIES

Oh, the addition of fruit to a savory meal makes my heart happy. The fruit adds sweetness, of course, but it's not too sweet, and crossing the traditional boundaries of what we think of as savory can be surprising, lovely, and, honestly, a little grown-up–feeling. Chicken is a blank canvas on which to paint a meal, and this one has so many notes—the crunchy hazelnuts, the sweet-and-sour cherries, the nutty quinoa, and the slight bite of the arugula. What a party of flavors!

Serves 2

¼ cup coarsely chopped hazelnuts

1 tablespoon extra-virgin olive oil, plus a drizzle for the arugula

2 chicken breasts (about 6 ounces each)

Kosher salt and freshly ground black pepper

1 cup fresh or frozen cherries, pitted and halved

1 teaspoon grated lime zest (from about ½ lime)

1 tablespoon fresh lime juice (from about ½ lime)

1 tablespoon balsamic vinegar, plus a drizzle for the arugula

½ cup quinoa

1 cup water

4 cups lightly packed arugula

¼ cup plain Greek yogurt

2 teaspoons honey

1. Heat a medium skillet over medium-high heat. Add the nuts and toast, stirring continuously, until they become fragrant and lightly brown, 2 to 4 minutes. Transfer to a small bowl and set aside.

2. Return the skillet to medium-high heat, add the oil and chicken, and sprinkle with a pinch of salt and pepper. Cook for 7 minutes on one side, then flip the breasts. After about 5 minutes, add the cherries and lime zest to the skillet and cook until the cherries are hot and the chicken is cooked through, 1 to 2 minutes more. Turn off the heat and add the lime juice, vinegar, and another sprinkle of salt and pepper. Move the chicken to a plate to let rest while assembling the rest of the dish.

3. While the chicken is cooking, make the quinoa: Bring the water to a boil in a small pot. Add the quinoa and a pinch of salt, cover, and reduce the heat to low. Simmer for 5 minutes and then turn off the heat. Set aside, covered, until the rest of the meal is ready.

4. To dress the arugula, put it in a medium bowl, lightly drizzle with olive oil and balsamic vinegar, sprinkle with salt and pepper, and toss well.

5. To assemble the dish, scoop the quinoa onto a platter or two plates. Add the dressed arugula and the chicken. Spoon the sauce over the chicken and top with the yogurt, the honey, and the nuts.

In the Pot

While a stew simmering all day on the stovetop
is one of the coziest things on the planet,
in a small space, the steam and the heat make
it less than practical. Then there's the fuel and
energy used to run the burner for several hours—
a minimalist kitchen might take the use of fuel
into account as well. Here, I've taken basic stew
and soup recipes and turned them into
quicker versions so that you don't end up
heating yourself out of the kitchen.

CHICKEN MURPHY, ANNIE-STYLE

This recipe originates with my friend Willette Brown of Union, Maine. It's been a loosely scripted recipe in her family for some time, and she tells me her husband gets a tiny bit grumpy if he doesn't get it every six weeks or so. I can see why. My version of it has become a favorite in our household as well.

While it already includes a carbohydrate in the form of potatoes, Willette sometimes serves it with rice or pasta. A salad never goes amiss with a meal like this either.

Serves 2

- 1 tablespoon extra-virgin olive oil
- 6 ounces boneless chicken thighs, cut into 1-inch cubes (about 2 thighs)
- 2 tablespoons bread crumbs
- 6 ounces white baby potatoes, halved (about 6 to 8 potatoes)
- 4 ounces mushrooms, quartered (about 1 cup)
- 1 medium onion, cut into 1-inch pieces (about 1 cup)
- 1 red bell pepper, cut into 1-inch pieces (about 1½ cups)
- 1½ teaspoons kosher salt

  Freshly ground black pepper
- 1 (14.5-ounce) can diced tomatoes
- ¾ cup chicken broth
- ¼ cup pickled hot banana pepper rings
- ¼ cup white wine
- 3 ounces Italian sausage, casing removed, broken into small pieces (about 1 link)

  Italian bread, for dunking

1. Heat the oil in a medium skillet over medium-high heat. Add the chicken and bread crumbs and cook for 7 to 10 minutes, until lightly browned.

2. Add the potatoes, mushrooms, onion, red bell pepper, salt, and a few grinds of pepper to the skillet. Sauté for 10 minutes. Then add the diced tomatoes, broth, banana peppers, wine, and sausage. Bring to a simmer, cover, and cook until the potatoes are tender, about 30 minutes.

3. Serve with good Italian bread for dunking in the stew.

BACON AND SAGE BEEF STEW

This one is a family favorite, and how could it not be? Bacon plus beef stew equals goodness. Serve it with homemade spaetzle, wide egg noodles, or mashed potatoes—your choice. Unlike many stews, this one does not contain potatoes, so it is easily frozen (potatoes turn mushy when defrosted).

Serves 2, generously

- 2 strips bacon, diced
- 1½ tablespoons all-purpose flour
- ½ teaspoon paprika

    Kosher salt and freshly ground black pepper

- 1 pound beef sirloin, cut into ¾-inch cubes
- 2 tablespoons extra-virgin olive oil
- 1½ cups carrot sticks, cut into 2-inch lengths (about 2 carrots)
- 1½ cups sliced onions (about 1 large onion)
- 2 cloves garlic, thinly sliced
- 1 large sage sprig, tied with a string
- 2 cups beef broth

    Spaetzle, egg noodles, or mashed potatoes, for serving

1. Heat a large skillet over medium-high heat. Add the bacon and fry until it is crispy. Transfer the bacon to a small bowl and scrape the fat out of the pan (save it for another recipe).

2. Mix the flour, paprika, a pinch of salt, and several grinds of pepper in a large bowl. Add the beef and toss to fully coat it with the flour mixture. Return the large skillet to medium-high heat. Add the beef and sear until the beef is browned on the outside but still tender on the inside, 3 to 4 minutes. Remove from the skillet to a plate.

3. Add the oil, carrots, onions, garlic, and sage to the skillet and sprinkle with salt and pepper. Reduce the heat to medium. Sauté the vegetables until the onions are soft and translucent and the carrots are tender, 7 to 10 minutes.

4. Pour the broth into the skillet and bring to a boil. Return the beef to the skillet to warm up for a minute or so. Serve the stew over spaetzle, egg noodles, or mashed potatoes, garnished with bacon.

COGNAC AND DIJON BEEF STROGANOFF WITH EGG NOODLES

Hello, elegant. Could a dish be any more classic or classy than one that involves Cognac and beef? Serve this dish with a special Cabernet Sauvignon, and maybe candles, too.

Serves 2

- 6 ounces egg noodles
- 1 (¾-pound) well-trimmed sirloin steak, cut into ¾-inch cubes
- 1 tablespoon all-purpose flour
- ½ teaspoon paprika
- ½ teaspoon kosher salt
  Freshly ground black pepper
- 1 tablespoon salted butter
- 1 cup diced onion (about 1 medium onion)
- 4 ounces mushrooms, quartered (about 1 cup)
- ½ cup chicken broth
- 1½ tablespoons Cognac or other brandy
- 1½ teaspoons Dijon mustard
- 2 tablespoons grated Parmesan cheese, for garnish

1. Bring a medium pot of salted water to a boil. Add the noodles and cook until al dente, according to the package instructions. Drain.

2. Meanwhile, combine the beef with the flour, paprika, salt, and several grinds of pepper in a small bowl and toss to coat.

3. Melt 1½ teaspoons of the butter in a medium stockpot over medium-high heat. Add the onion and cook until translucent, 7 to 10 minutes. Add the floured beef, the mushrooms, and the remaining 1½ teaspoons butter and cook until the beef is well browned on the outside but still tender on the inside, 4 to 5 minutes.

4. Add the broth, Cognac, and mustard to the pot. Bring to a boil, scraping any browned bits from the bottom of the pan, and then remove from the heat.

5. To serve, transfer the egg noodles to a platter or two plates. Spoon the beef mixture over the noodles and garnish with Parmesan.

BACK-TO-YOUR-CHILDHOOD TOMATO BASIL SOUP WITH GRILLED CHEESE

When I was growing up, I loved grilled cheese and tomato soup—especially in the winter after a day of playing outside. We'd come indoors, rosy-cheeked and happy for a mug of something warm to wrap our hands around. We loved to dip the edges of our sandwiches in a dollop of Dijon. My own children, now nearly adults, still do the same.

The recipe below calls for dried basil, but fresh basil, when available, is delicious. Also, in summertime, thick soup isn't as satisfying, so you may want to leave out the flour for a brighter and slightly thinner soup.

The quality of the tomatoes in this recipe matters a good deal since they are the centerpiece. If you have home-canned tomatoes, frozen whole tomatoes (skins removed), or fresh tomatoes straight from the garden or farmers' market, this is the place to use them. If not, a quality canned tomato, such as San Marzanos, will work perfectly well.

Serves 2

TOMATO SOUP

- 1 tablespoon extra-virgin olive oil
- ½ cup diced onion (about 1 small onion)
- Kosher salt and freshly ground black pepper
- 1 tablespoon minced garlic (about 1 clove)
- 1 tablespoon dried basil
- ½ teaspoon paprika
- 1 teaspoon all-purpose flour
- 1 cup chicken broth
- ¼ cup white wine
- 1 (16-ounce) can diced tomatoes or 2 cups diced fresh tomatoes (about 2 tomatoes)
- 2 tablespoons minced scallions, for garnish
- 2 tablespoons crème fraîche, for garnish

GRILLED CHEESE

- 2 tablespoons salted butter, softened
- 4 slices peasant bread or sourdough bread
- 4 ounces extra-sharp cheddar cheese, sliced
- 2 ounces Monterey Jack cheese, sliced
- 2 teaspoons Dijon mustard, for serving

Recipe continues on next page

1. To make the soup, heat the oil in a large stockpot over medium heat. Add the onion and sauté for 7 to 10 minutes, until translucent. Add a pinch of salt, a few grinds of black pepper, and the garlic, basil, and paprika and sauté for another 2 minutes or so, stirring frequently.

2. Add the flour to the pot, stirring until it is well incorporated. Then add the broth and wine and stir well again. Add the tomatoes and bring to a boil, then reduce the heat and let simmer, uncovered, for 30 minutes.

3. When the soup is almost done simmering, make the grilled cheese sandwiches: Heat a large griddle over medium-low heat. Meanwhile, butter one side of each slice of bread. Make sure the butter reaches all the way to the edges. Place two slices on the griddle, buttered side down, and place the cheese slices on top. Top with the remaining slices of bread, buttered side up. Grill for 4 to 6 minutes on each side, until the bread is golden brown and crispy and the cheese is completely melted and gooey in the center. Remove from the griddle to a cutting board.

4. Ladle the soup into bowls and garnish with scallions and crème fraîche. Slice the sandwiches in half and serve with Dijon on the side for dipping.

CREAMY PUMPKIN ALMOND SOUP

The blend of spices in this recipe is similar to berbere, an Ethiopian spice mix that can be tricky to find in grocery stores. It lends a special depth and richness that sets this soup apart from others.

Serves 2

- 1 tablespoon coconut oil
- 1 cup diced onion (about 1 medium onion)
- 8 ounces pumpkin (or butternut squash) flesh, cut into 1-inch cubes, or 1 cup canned pumpkin purée
- ½ teaspoon kosher salt
- ½ teaspoon paprika
- ¼ teaspoon allspice
- ¼ teaspoon ground cardamom
- ¼ teaspoon ground cinnamon
- ¼ teaspoon ground ginger
- 1 teaspoon minced garlic (about 1 clove)
- 1 tablespoon grated fresh ginger
- 1 cup chicken broth
- 1 cup unsweetened plain oat (or coconut or almond) milk
- ½ cup plus 2 tablespoons blanched slivered almonds
- 2 tablespoons unsweetened coconut flakes
- 2 tablespoons thinly sliced scallions, green part only (reserve the white parts for another recipe)
- Several sprigs of fresh cilantro

1. Heat the coconut oil in a medium pot over medium-high heat. Add the onion, pumpkin, salt, paprika, allspice, cardamom, cinnamon, and ground ginger and sauté, stirring often, for 15 minutes, until the onion is translucent and the pumpkin has broken up. Add the garlic and fresh ginger and sauté for 1 minute more. Then add the broth, milk, and ½ cup of the almonds. Bring to a boil, then reduce the heat and let simmer, uncovered, for 10 minutes.

2. Transfer the soup to a blender or use an immersion blender. Purée until smooth. If you don't have either tool, don't worry; your soup will be a bit more rustic, but just as delicious.

3. Heat a small skillet over medium-high heat. Add the remaining 2 tablespoons almonds and coconut flakes and toast for 2 to 3 minutes, stirring nearly continuously, until lightly browned and fragrant.

4. Serve the soup hot, garnished with toasted almonds and coconut, scallions, and cilantro.

LENTILS WITH ROASTED CAULIFLOWER AND CARROTS, BEET HUMMUS, AND PARSLEY RELISH

Roasted cauliflower is about the best thing on the planet. When the sugars in this mild vegetable caramelize, something magical and delicious occurs. The resulting flavor is deeply satisfying, nearly meat-like, and just as delicious.

Serves 2

CAULIFLOWER AND CARROTS

- 1 tablespoon coconut oil
- ½ head cauliflower, cut into 1-inch florets (about 3 cups)
- 6 small carrots, cut in half lengthwise (or 2 large carrots cut into 3-inch sticks)

  Kosher salt and freshly ground black pepper

LENTILS

- ½ teaspoon ground cumin
- 2 cups chicken or vegetable broth
- ⅔ cup dried Le Puy or green lentils
- 1 whole clove garlic

BEET HUMMUS

- 1 medium beet, trimmed
- ½ cup canned garbanzo beans
- 2 tablespoons tahini
- 1 tablespoon fresh lemon juice
- 1 teaspoon tamari

  Freshly ground black pepper

PARSLEY RELISH

- ½ cup minced fresh flat-leaf parsley
- 1 tablespoon extra-virgin olive oil
- ½ teaspoon minced garlic (about ½ clove)
- ¼ teaspoon grated lemon zest
- 1 teaspoon fresh lemon juice

  Pinch of kosher salt

1. To make the cauliflower and carrots, heat the coconut oil in a medium skillet over medium-high heat. Add the cauliflower and carrots to the skillet and sprinkle with a fat pinch of salt and several grinds of pepper. Cover the skillet and sear the vegetables for 20 to 25 minutes. Reduce the heat to low when they have nicely browned but still need a little more time to become tender.

2. To make the lentils, heat a small pot over medium-high heat. Add the cumin and toast it until it becomes fragrant, about 30 seconds. Add the broth, lentils, and garlic. Bring to a boil, then reduce the heat, cover, and let simmer for 15 to 20 minutes, until the lentils are tender and have fully absorbed the broth.

3. To make the hummus, cover the beet with water in a small pot and bring to a boil. Boil for 20 to 30 minutes, until the beet is tender when pierced with a knife, and then drain. When the beet is cool enough to handle, peel it and cut it into large cubes. Mash the beet cubes with the garbanzo beans, tahini, lemon juice, tamari, and several grinds of pepper in a small bowl with a potato masher, or pulse everything in a food processor.

4. To make the parsley relish, combine the parsley, olive oil, garlic, lemon zest, lemon juice, and salt in a small bowl and mix well.

5. To serve, layer the vegetables on the lentils and top with the hummus and parsley relish.

Switch It Up!

MORE WAYS TO USE PARSLEY RELISH

Swirled into a white bean soup | Dotted on top of a chili- or cumin-rubbed grilled steak | Tossed with fresh tomatoes, capers, and pasta

YELLOW DAL, TOMATOES, AND SPINACH

Dal is such comfort food for me, in the same way that polenta and oatmeal are. Maybe it's a texture thing. In any case, the acid in the tomatoes and yogurt balances beautifully with the bright spinach and cilantro. If you can't find yellow lentils, the more common red lentils will work perfectly well.

Serves 2

YELLOW DAL

1¼ cups chicken or vegetable broth

½ cup yellow lentils

1 (½-inch) piece fresh ginger

½ teaspoon ground cumin

½ teaspoon mustard seeds

Kosher salt

TOMATOES AND SPINACH

1 tablespoon unsalted butter

1 cup sliced onions (about 1 medium onion)

2 tablespoons grated fresh ginger

1 tablespoon minced garlic (about 3 cloves)

1 teaspoon ground cumin

1 teaspoon garam masala

Kosher salt

1½ cups diced plum tomatoes (about 2 tomatoes)

2 cups lightly packed spinach leaves

Handful of fresh cilantro leaves

Low-fat or whole-milk plain yogurt

1. To make the dal, combine the broth, lentils, whole piece of ginger, cumin, and mustard seeds in a small pot. Bring to a boil, then reduce the heat and let simmer, covered, for 10 to 15 minutes, stirring occasionally, until the lentils are tender and begin to get mushy. Keep a careful watch; you might need to add a little water if the dal gets very thick. When the lentils are done cooking, season them with salt to taste (adding salt earlier will make them tough). Remove the piece of ginger.

2. To prepare the tomatoes, melt the butter in a medium skillet over medium-high heat. Add the onions and sauté for 5 to 6 minutes, until the onions begin to soften. Add the ginger, garlic, cumin, garam masala, and a fat pinch of kosher salt and sauté for another 2 to 3 minutes, until the onions are translucent. Add the tomatoes and cook until they are soft, about 3 minutes.

3. Arrange the spinach on a serving platter or in two bowls and top with the dal, the tomato mixture, fresh cilantro, and a dollop of yogurt.

SPINACH BALLS WITH SEARED ONION MARINARA SAUCE AND ZUCCHINI

For young kids, this recipe is a sure thing served with pasta, but using zucchini instead creates a lighter and healthier version that satisfies those looking for something less carb-heavy. There's no need to own a spiralizer for the zucchini (we've already had the mono-tool talk). Either purchase the zucchini from the store already spiralized or, instead, make long ribbons with a vegetable peeler.

The sauce is a simple standby and easy to embellish. If you'd like it to be less rustic or to use it as a dipping sauce, purée it in a small food processor. It is an excellent complement to the spinach balls. The full recipe uses an entire package of frozen spinach and results in 10 extra spinach balls that you can enjoy another time (see the suggestions on page 180). They are delicious!

Serves 2

SPINACH BALLS (MAKES 20 BALLS)

- 1 tablespoon salted butter
- ½ cup grated onion (about 1 small onion)
- 1 (16-ounce) package frozen chopped spinach, defrosted
- 1 cup bread crumbs
- ¼ cup grated Parmesan cheese
- 1 egg
- Kosher salt and freshly ground black pepper

MARINARA SAUCE AND ZUCCHINI

- 2 tablespoons extra-virgin olive oil
- 1 medium onion, sliced into 4 wide rounds
- Kosher salt and freshly ground black pepper
- 1 tablespoon minced garlic (about 3 cloves)
- 1 (16-ounce) can crushed San Marzano tomatoes
- 3 cups spiralized zucchini (about 1 zucchini cut into very thin strips)
- ¼ cup grated Parmesan cheese

Recipe continues on next page

1. Preheat the oven to 350°F (180°C). Line a baking sheet with parchment paper.

2. To make the spinach balls, melt the butter in a medium saucepan over medium-high heat. Add the grated onion and sauté until translucent, about 5 minutes. Remove from the heat and stir in the spinach, bread crumbs, Parmesan, egg, a fat pinch of salt, and several grinds of pepper.

3. Form the spinach mixture into 1-inch balls and place on the prepared baking sheet. Bake for 30 minutes, or until the centers are hot and a crust has formed on the outside.

4. To make the sauce, heat 1 tablespoon of the oil in a medium skillet over medium heat. Carefully lay the onion rounds in the skillet, sprinkle with salt and pepper, and cook for 10 to 15 minutes, turning once or twice. Be sure not to rush this stage, as it's what gives the sauce its yummy goodness. When the onions are soft and nicely caramelized, transfer them to a cutting board and dice them.

5. Return the onions to the skillet, add the garlic, and sauté for 30 seconds to 1 minute, until the garlic is fragrant. Add the tomatoes and bring to a boil, then reduce the heat and let simmer, uncovered, for 20 to 30 minutes, until the sauce thickens slightly.

6. To cook the zucchini, heat the remaining 1 tablespoon oil in a medium skillet over medium-high heat. Add the zucchini, sprinkle with salt and pepper, and sauté for 2 minutes, or until the zucchini is heated through.

7. To serve, divide the zucchini evenly between two bowls. Ladle the sauce over the zucchini, top each bowl with five spinach balls, and garnish with Parmesan.

Switch It Up!

MORE WAYS TO USE SPINACH BALLS

In chicken soup with Parmesan cheese | With seared kale, green beans, and garlic | With roasted tomato halves | Baked with cream, garlic, and black pepper

SUMMER MINESTRONE SOUP

This soup is quick and easy and reminds me of that time of year when the garden bursts with produce and all of these fabulous vegetables are ready to harvest. It's summer in a bowl—but available any time of the year—and as delightful as a sunny day in the garden.

Serves 2

- 1 tablespoon extra-virgin olive oil
- 1 cup diced onion (about 1 medium onion)
- ½ cup diced carrot (about ½ carrot)
- 1 cup diced zucchini (about 1 small zucchini)
- ½ cup chopped green beans, cut into 1-inch pieces (about 2 ounces)
- 1 tablespoon minced garlic (about 3 cloves)
- 1 teaspoon dried Italian seasoning (or ½ teaspoon dried basil plus ½ teaspoon dried oregano)
- ½ teaspoon kosher salt
- Freshly ground black pepper
- 1 ripe tomato
- 2 cups chicken broth
- 1 cup canned cannellini beans
- ¼ cup orecchiette or orzo pasta
- Several fresh basil leaves, torn into pieces
- 2 tablespoons grated Parmesan cheese, for garnish

1. Heat the oil in a medium pot over medium-high heat. Add the onion and carrot and sauté for 7 to 10 minutes, until the onions are soft and translucent. Add the zucchini, green beans, garlic, Italian seasoning, salt, and several grinds of pepper. Let cook, stirring occasionally.

2. Stand a grater with large holes in a bowl. Cut the tomato in half. Holding the curved outside of each half in the palm of your hand, grate the inside of the tomato until all that is left is the skin. Discard the skin and add the tomato pulp to the pot.

3. Add the broth, cannellini beans, and pasta to the pot. Bring to a boil, then reduce the heat and simmer, uncovered, for 8 to 10 minutes, until the pasta is cooked through.

4. Ladle the soup into two serving bowls. Serve garnished with torn basil leaves and Parmesan.

MUSSELS BOUILLABAISSE WITH ROUILLE

Bouillabaisse is essentially a seafood stew. Without the traditional Pernod (an anise-flavored liqueur) and saffron, it's a lovely, simple way to enjoy mussels with some crusty bread to sop up the broth. But when Pernod and saffron are part of the package, suddenly what seemed wonderful becomes amazing.

   Rouille is magic sauce and can be drizzled into the broth, used as a dipping sauce, or spread on a baguette. If you aren't feeling up to the bouillabaisse, you can always prepare the mussels in a traditional butter, garlic, and white wine broth and serve them with rouille.

ROUILLE

- ½ cup canned roasted red pepper, drained, or ½ roasted red pepper, skin and seeds removed
- 3 tablespoons lightly packed fresh flat-leaf parsley
- 1 egg yolk
- 1 teaspoon minced garlic (about 1 clove)
- 1½ teaspoons fresh lemon juice
- ¼ teaspoon kosher salt
- 2 tablespoons extra-virgin olive oil

MUSSELS BOUILLABAISSE

- 1 tablespoon extra-virgin olive oil
- ½ cup diced carrot
- ½ cup diced fennel
- ½ cup well-cleaned diced leeks
- ½ cup diced onion (about 1 small onion)
-   Pinch of kosher salt
-   Tiny pinch of red pepper flakes
- 1 teaspoon minced garlic (about 1 clove)
- 1 cup clam stock or chicken broth
- ¼ cup white wine
-   Pinch of saffron threads
- 1 pound mussels, cleaned and beards removed
- 1½ tablespoons Pernod (or other anisette liquor)
-   Baguette, for dunking

1. To make the rouille, mash the roasted pepper, parsley, egg yolk, garlic, lemon juice, and salt with a potato masher in a small bowl, or pulse everything in a food processor. Slowly whisk in the oil, barely dribbling it in at the beginning and then building to a slow, steady stream. If the sauce is too thick, add a little of the bouillabaisse broth once it's made.

2. To make the bouillabaisse, heat the oil in a medium saucepan over medium-high heat. Add the carrot, fennel, leeks, onion, salt, and red pepper flakes and sauté for 10 minutes, or until the onions are translucent and the rest of the vegetables are soft.

3. Add the garlic and sauté for 1 minute. Then add the stock, wine, and saffron and bring to a boil. Add the mussels and Pernod, cover, and boil for 2 to 3 minutes. The mussels are done when they open completely. Remove any that don't open at all. Serve immediately, with rouille and a baguette for dunking.

Switch It Up!

MORE WAYS TO USE ROUILLE

Spread on toast with grated Fontina for an open-faced melt | Swirled into potato leek soup | Added to scallops sautéed in butter and garlic and served over polenta

CHAPTER 7

FROM THE OVEN . . . OR TOASTER OVEN

If your kitchen doesn't have an oven, wait—
don't skip over this section. These recipes can all be
re-created in a skillet (see page 22), on a grill,
or in a toaster oven. (With the baked items, for the
most part, an oven or toaster oven is necessary.)
When you're cooking with a toaster oven, note that
the cooking time or baking time is typically reduced
by one-third, but each toaster oven will be different,
so you'll need to play around with yours to sort out
exactly what changes you need to make. Fear not;
most anything that can be made in a conventional oven
can also be made in a toaster oven.

CARAMELIZED SHALLOT, SPINACH, AND COMTÉ TARTLET

Cooking in a small space can require some ingenuity and creativity. When that small space then also tilts, as, say, on a sailboat, then the planning, patience, and forethought need to kick into high gear. All this is to say that this wonderful tart is best made when the vessel is at anchor or the RV is not on the road. The bottom of your oven will thank you.

This recipe will work in any small baking pan. I use a 7-inch round tart pan, but a 9- by 9-inch baking pan or a pie plate would do.

Serves 2

CRUST

¾ cup all-purpose flour

Pinch of table salt

4 tablespoons unsalted butter, chilled and cut into ½-inch pieces

4 tablespoons ice-cold water

FILLING

1 tablespoon extra-virgin olive oil

1½ cups thinly sliced shallots (about 6 shallots)

Kosher salt and freshly ground black pepper

1 cup lightly packed baby spinach

2 eggs

⅓ cup plus 1 tablespoon half-and-half

2 ounces Comté cheese, grated (about ½ cup)

1 teaspoon fresh thyme

1. To make the crust, combine the flour and salt in a medium bowl. Use your hands to press the butter into the flour mixture until it has the consistency of a coarse meal, or pulse the butter and flour in a food processor to the same consistency. Add the water and mix until combined. If the dough is too dry, add more water 1 teaspoon at a time until you can form it into a ball. Press the dough into a disk, wrap in plastic wrap, and chill for 30 minutes.

2. Preheat the oven to 400°F (200°C).

3. Dust the surface of a counter with flour and roll the dough out onto it to ¼-inch thickness. Press the dough into a 7-inch round tart pan. Lightly poke the crust all over with a fork. Cover the crust with parchment paper, fill the pan with dry beans or pie weights, and bake for 20 minutes, or until the crust is a light golden brown. Remove the crust from the oven. Reduce the oven temperature to 325°F (170°C).

4. To make the filling, heat the oil in a small skillet over medium-high heat. Add the shallots, sprinkle with salt and pepper, and sauté until the shallots are caramelized, about 10 minutes. When the shallots are done, add the spinach, stir to combine, and remove the skillet from the heat.

5. Whisk the eggs, half-and-half, and a pinch of salt and pepper together in a small bowl.

6. Distribute the shallots and spinach over the prebaked crust. Pour in the egg mixture and sprinkle with the Comté and thyme. Bake for 15 to 20 minutes, until the center is just barely cooked and still wiggly. Serve hot or at room temperature.

ROASTED KALE, MUSHROOMS, ONION, AND BELL PEPPER WITH BLUE CHEESE

This dish embodies the sort of comfort food that I love best: all kinds of flavor, easy to make, tons of veggies. It needs only a salad and maybe some bread to make a perfect meal.

If you've ever made kale chips, you know that roasted kale is wonderful when the leaves are perfectly dry. Even a tiny bit of moisture creates steam, though, which in turn leads to a completely different texture, minus the crispiness that I adore. So be sure that your kale is absolutely dry before you roast it.

Serves 2

1 medium onion, cut into 1-inch wedges

1 red or orange bell pepper, cut into 1-inch pieces

8 whole button mushrooms

3 tablespoons extra-virgin olive oil

Kosher salt and freshly ground black pepper

4 ounces kale, coarsely chopped (about 1 small bunch or 4 cups)

2 ounces blue cheese, crumbled (about ½ cup)

Slices of focaccia, for serving

1. Preheat the oven to 450°F (230°C).

2. Heat a medium ovenproof skillet over medium-high heat. Add the onions, bell pepper, and mushrooms, drizzle with 2 tablespoons of the oil, and sprinkle with a pinch of salt and several grinds of pepper. Cook for 3 to 4 minutes, until the vegetables are hot, and then transfer the skillet to the oven. Roast for 30 to 40 minutes, until the vegetables are browned on the edges and tender in the center.

3. Put the kale in a medium bowl, drizzle remaining 1 tablespoon oil over it, and rub the oil into the greens with your hands. Lightly sprinkle with salt and pepper and toss to combine. Transfer the kale to the skillet, mounding it up on top. Roast for 10 minutes, or until the kale is crispy.

4. Remove the skillet from the oven. Crumble the blue cheese over the kale and serve with big hunks of focaccia.

ROASTED BUTTERNUT SQUASH WITH PECANS AND CAMBOZOLA

In this salad, the pecans and Cambozola, a creamy, Brie-like blue cheese, come together to create a salty-sweet richness that needs no other protein to be satisfying as a meal all on its own. Change it up a bit with walnuts and Gorgonzola or hazelnuts and Fontina. Allspice or ancho chile powder could replace the cumin.

Serves 2

1 pound butternut squash, cut into ¾-inch cubes (about 4 cups)

1 tablespoon plus 1 teaspoon extra-virgin olive oil

Kosher salt and freshly ground black pepper

½ cup pecans

½ teaspoon ground cumin

½ teaspoon sugar

2 ounces Cambozola cheese

4 cups lightly packed arugula

1 teaspoon fresh lemon juice

1. Preheat the oven to 400°F (200°C).

2. Coat the squash with ½ teaspoon of the oil, sprinkle with a pinch of salt and several grinds of pepper, and roast on a baking sheet for 45 minutes, or until the squash is tender and starting to develop some crispy edges.

3. Combine the pecans in a bowl with ½ teaspoon of the oil, the cumin, and the sugar and toss to coat. Add to the pan with the squash and roast for 10 minutes.

4. Slice the Cambozola thinly and dot pieces of it all over the squash and pecans. Return the pan to the oven for another 5 minutes.

5. Toss the arugula with the remaining 1 tablespoon oil and the lemon juice, sprinkle with salt and pepper, and top with the roasted squash mixture. Serve immediately.

RAS EL HANOUT CARROTS over QUINOA, YOGURT, and GARBANZO BEANS

Thinking about vegetables as the main characters rather than sidekicks is, to me, part of a successful small-kitchen strategy. Doing so shifts the focus from the traditional categories of meat, starch, and vegetable to a conversation about the meal as a whole.

Ras el hanout is a Moroccan blend of sometimes more than 30 different spices and herbs, with a focus on ginger, cardamom, mace, and cinnamon. It's readily available in the spice section of most grocery stores, but if you have trouble finding it, try garam masala, harissa, or a curry blend instead.

Adding greens to a meal never goes amiss. This one would welcome spinach tossed and wilted in the quinoa or kale sautéed with garlic.

Serves 2

2 large carrots, cut into 3-inch sticks

1 small red onion, cut into 1-inch wedges

1 teaspoon extra-virgin olive oil

1 teaspoon ras el hanout

Kosher salt and freshly ground black pepper

1 cup canned garbanzo beans, rinsed well and patted dry

½ teaspoon ground cumin

1 cup water

½ cup quinoa

¼ cup plain Greek yogurt

Lemon wedges, for serving

1. Preheat the oven to 400°F (200°C).

2. Toss the carrots and onion with the oil, ras el hanout, a pinch of salt, and several grinds of pepper. Spread on a small baking pan and roast for 30 minutes.

3. Meanwhile, combine the garbanzo beans with the cumin in a small bowl, sprinkle with salt and pepper, and toss to mix. When the carrots have roasted for 30 minutes, add the beans to the baking pan and roast for another 15 to 20 minutes, until the carrots are tender.

4. To make the quinoa, bring the water to a boil and add the quinoa and a pinch of salt. Cover and reduce the heat to low. Simmer for 5 minutes and then turn off the heat. Set aside, covered, until the rest of the meal is ready.

5. To serve, arrange the quinoa on a platter and top with the roasted carrots, onions, and beans. Add small dollops of yogurt and serve with lemon wedges to squeeze over everything.

CARAMELIZED ONION, MUSHROOM, AND TURKEY MEATLOAF WITH BOURSIN MASHERS

This is a swanked-up version of my mom's beef meatloaf recipe. As a little girl, I loved the leftover meatloaf sandwiches more than the meal itself.

Creating a free-form loaf eliminates the need for a loaf pan and has the added benefit of creating more crust around the exterior. The caramelized onions and mushrooms give richness and moisture to the turkey, which, because of its low-fat content, can sometimes be dry.

For the Boursin mashers, I like to use baby potatoes because the skins aren't so developed that you need to peel them. Should baby potatoes not be available to you, do take the time to peel, since the skins are too tough to be pleasant.

Serves 2 (with enough leftovers to make 2 great sandwiches the next day)

MEATLOAF

- 1 tablespoon extra-virgin olive oil
- 1½ cups sliced onions (about 1 large onion)
- 1½ cups minced button mushrooms (about 4 ounces)
- ¾ teaspoon kosher salt
- Freshly ground black pepper
- 1 pound ground turkey
- ½ cup old-fashioned rolled oats or bread crumbs
- 1 egg
- 3 tablespoons ketchup
- 2 tablespoons milk

BOURSIN MASHERS

- 12 ounces baby Yukon Gold potatoes (about 20 potatoes)
- 1 tablespoon salted butter
- 3 tablespoons Boursin (or Boursin-like) cheese
- Kosher salt and freshly ground black pepper
- Splash of milk, if needed

1. Preheat the oven to 375°F (190°C).

2. Heat the oil in a skillet over medium-high heat. Add the onions and sauté for 5 minutes. Add the mushrooms, ¼ teaspoon of the salt, and several grinds of pepper. Reduce the heat to medium-low and cook for 10 minutes, or until the onions caramelize. Take the time to make sure the onions and mushrooms are fully cooked and caramelized, since this is where all the flavor is developed.

3. Transfer the caramelized onion mixture to a large bowl. Add the turkey, oats, egg, ketchup, milk, remaining ½ teaspoon salt, and a pinch of pepper. Mix with your hands until fully incorporated.

4. Lay a piece of parchment paper or aluminum foil on a baking sheet. Shape the turkey mixture into a loaf on the parchment. Bake for 1 hour, or until an instant-read thermometer registers an internal temperature of 165°F (74°C). Let rest at least 5 minutes before serving.

5. While the meatloaf is baking, prepare the potatoes. Cover the potatoes with water in a medium pot and salt the water liberally. Bring to a boil, then reduce the heat and let simmer for 20 minutes, or until the potatoes are tender when poked in the center with a fork. Drain and transfer back into the pot.

6. Use a potato masher to mash the potatoes. Add the butter and Boursin, season with salt and pepper to taste, and mix well. Add milk, if needed, to loosen the potatoes.

7. To serve, cut the meatloaf into ¾-inch slices and serve hot with the mashed potatoes.

SWEET POTATO WITH SPINACH, GOAT'S MILK CREAM CHEESE, WALNUTS, AND POACHED EGGS

Sweet potatoes are fine when they are cooked just until they are soft in consistency. But they become truly sublime when the starches are allowed the time to caramelize. In this dish, that sweet caramelization is so happy with the garlicky spinach, creamy goat cheese, and slightly bitter walnuts. Heaven on a plate is worth the wait.

The egg-poaching instructions here are simplified. If you'd like more detail, see page 77.

Serves 2

- 1 large sweet potato, cut in half lengthwise
- 2 teaspoons avocado oil

  Kosher salt and freshly ground black pepper
- 2 teaspoons minced garlic (about 2 cloves)
- 4 cups lightly packed baby spinach
- 3 tablespoons coarsely chopped walnuts
- 2–4 eggs (depending on how hungry you are)

  Splash of white vinegar
- 1 ounce goat's milk cream cheese or crème fraîche

1. Preheat the oven to 375°F (190°C).

2. Rub the sweet potato halves with 1 teaspoon of the avocado oil, set them with their cut side facing up in a small ovenproof skillet, and sprinkle with salt and pepper. Roast for 1 hour and 15 minutes, or until the sweet potato is soft in the center and browning on the edges.

Recipe continues on next page

3. Remove the sweet potato halves from the skillet and set the skillet over medium-high heat. Add the remaining 1 teaspoon oil and the garlic and sauté for 30 seconds to 1 minute, until the garlic is fragrant. Add the spinach and cook, turning with tongs, for 30 seconds, or until it is just wilted. Remove the spinach from the skillet.

4. Return the skillet to medium heat, add the walnuts, and toast for 1 to 2 minutes, until they begin to brown a little. Keep a close eye on them to prevent scorching. When they're toasted, remove them from the skillet and let cool.

5. To poach the eggs, fill a small saucepan with water and add a fat pinch of salt and a splash of vinegar. Bring almost to a simmer and hold it there. Gently swirl the water in one direction and then carefully break the eggs into the simmering water. When the egg whites are cooked through but the yolks are not, somewhere in the range of 4 to 5 minutes, remove the eggs from the water with a slotted spoon, dabbing the bottom of the spoon on a towel to absorb any water.

6. Return the sweet potatoes to the skillet and, using a fork, fluff the center of each half to make a well for the eggs. Gently transfer each egg to the well of a sweet potato half. Sprinkle with salt and pepper. Nestle the spinach next to the potatoes. Add a dollop of goat's milk cream cheese, top with the toasted walnuts, and serve immediately.

LIME AND SWEET CHILI CORNISH GAME HEN WITH BABY BOK CHOY AND SCALLIONS

Cornish game hens are especially suited to a small kitchen, where their diminutive size allows them to be cooked even in a toaster oven. In my house, one hen split in half is enough for two people. If you prefer a larger portion, however, it's easy enough to cook two side by side. Just double the marinade to accommodate the change.

Serves 2

1 tablespoon grated fresh ginger

2 teaspoons grated garlic (about 2 cloves)

1 tablespoon fresh lime juice (from about ½ lime)

1 tablespoon sweet chili sauce

1 tablespoon tamari

1 Cornish game hen (a little over 1 pound)

¾ cup jasmine rice

1½ cups water

Kosher salt

1 tablespoon peanut oil

6–8 whole scallion whites, root ends removed (reserve the green tops for another recipe)

1 head baby bok choy, cut in half lengthwise

1 large clove garlic, sliced

Drizzle of sesame oil

2 lime wedges

1. Preheat the oven to 375°F (190°C).

2. Whisk the ginger, garlic, lime juice, sweet chili sauce, and tamari together in a small bowl. Rub the mixture all over the hen, inside and out. Line a small pan with parchment paper and place the hen on the paper. Roast for 1 hour, or until an instant-read thermometer registers an internal temperature of 170°F (77°C) for the thighs.

3. While the hen is roasting, make the rice: Combine the rice, water, and a fat pinch of salt in a medium saucepan. Bring to a boil, then reduce the heat and let simmer, covered, for 15 minutes, or until the rice is tender. Remove from the heat and set aside, covered.

4. Heat the peanut oil in a small skillet over medium-high heat. Add the scallions and the bok choy, cut side down. Sprinkle the scallions with salt. Sear the scallions for 5 to 7 minutes, turning occasionally, then remove them from the skillet. Turn the bok choy over.

5. Reduce the heat to medium-low and add the garlic slices to the skillet with the bok choy. Drizzle the garlic with a little sesame oil and cook, stirring continuously for about 1 minute, until the garlic is nicely browned. Remove the garlic from the skillet and sprinkle with a tiny pinch of salt. Cover the skillet and let the bok choy cook for another 3 to 4 minutes, until the center is tender.

6. To serve, cut the hen in half through the breast bone. Transfer to a platter with the rice, bok choy, scallions, and garlic. Drizzle the pan juice from roasting the hen over the bok choy. Garnish with lime wedges.

HARISSA AND LEMON CORNISH GAME HEN WITH CARROTS, PARSNIPS, AND RED ONION

To give this dish a little extra decadence, add a bit of sour cream or crème fraîche to the sauce at the very end. Or, for a brighter flavor, mince some cilantro and scallions and whisk the herbs in with the harissa and lemon. If you prefer a larger portion than half a hen, you can cook two side by side.

Serves 2

2 tablespoons harissa paste

Kosher salt

1 Cornish game hen (a little over 1 pound)

1 lemon, cut into wedges

3 large carrots, cut into 3-inch sticks

3 parsnips, cut into 3-inch sticks

1 red onion, cut into 1-inch wedges

1 tablespoon extra-virgin olive oil

1. Preheat the oven to 375°F (190°C).

2. Rub 1 tablespoon of harissa and a pinch of salt all over the hen, inside and out. Line a roasting pan with parchment paper and place the hen on the paper. Set one of the lemon wedges aside, and then arrange the rest of the lemon, together with the carrots, parsnips, and onion, on the pan. Drizzle with the oil and sprinkle with salt. Roast for 1 hour, or until an instant-read thermometer registers an internal temperature of 170°F (77°C) for the thighs and the vegetables are tender.

3. To serve, cut the hen in half through the breast bone to make two servings. Transfer the roasted vegetables and lemon wedges to a serving platter and set the halved hen on top. Pour any pan juices into a small bowl. (If there aren't any pan juices, add ¼ cup water to the roasting pan and rub all the roasty bits off the bottom.) Add the remaining 1 tablespoon harissa to the pan juices, squeeze in the juice from the reserved lemon wedge, and whisk together. Serve in a ramekin.

CHAPTER 8

DESSERT IN A MUG AND MORE

The desserts in this chapter are
intended to be made in Mason jars, juice glasses,
mugs, espresso cups, and other containers
that any kitchen will already have on hand.
Ideally, these containers wouldn't be extra ones
that sit on the shelf and come out for special occasions,
but instead containers that can do double or
triple duty to serve different purposes. One moment
they could be holding your morning juice,
the next an evening cocktail, and then, as any good
workhorse will do, they might transition
to cradling a lovely dessert.

GINGER and BLACKBERRY CRÈME BRÛLÉE

My longtime mentor, a chef born and raised in Switzerland, taught me how to make crème brûlée in his tiny restaurant kitchen in Midcoast Maine. We stood side by side for three years, working together to plate meal after meal for the diners on the other side of the kitchen wall. It was always his job to "torch" the brûlées, and it wasn't until my second year that I graduated to that responsibility—he really liked each one to be perfect.

If you don't have a small torch, skip it, and just enjoy this dessert as a delicious pudding. Leftover egg whites from this recipe can get a second chance with either Coconut Macaroons (page 212) or Strawberry and Lemon Pavlova (page 210), or you can add them to an omelet the following morning.

Want to serve more than two? The ratios in this recipe remain the same as it is increased: 1 egg yolk per ½ cup cream.

Serves 2

1 cup heavy cream

1 vanilla bean, split and scraped

1 teaspoon grated fresh ginger

1 teaspoon cornstarch

2 tablespoons sugar

2 egg yolks

2 teaspoons minced crystallized ginger

4 tablespoons confectioners' sugar

6 blackberries

1. Heat the cream, vanilla bean (pod and scraped seeds), fresh ginger, and cornstarch in a small saucepan over high heat. In 4 to 5 minutes, when the cream comes to a boil (be careful because it seems to take forever and then happens all at once), remove from the heat and let sit for 15 minutes.

2. Whisk the sugar and the egg yolks together in a medium bowl until the mixture lightens and begins to thicken, 2 to 3 minutes. Then strain the cream into the egg mixture, discarding the vanilla bean pod and the ginger.

3. Transfer the cream mixture to the pan and add the crystallized ginger. Heat over medium-high heat, stirring constantly. Remove from the heat when the mixture thickens and is just about to boil, 2 to 3 minutes. You should see a little steam coming off the mixture.

4. Transfer to two shallow ramekins and refrigerate for at least 4 hours and up to 3 days.

5. When you're ready to serve, dust the confectioners' sugar over the cream. Using a torch, melt the sugar to form a crispy top. Top with the blackberries and serve immediately.

LEMON POPPY SEED BLUEBERRY TRIFLE

Normally, trifle is made with leftover cake that's drizzled with syrup and alcohol and topped with juicy fruit and luscious cream. Given that many small kitchens, for one reason or another, don't always have the capacity for baking, leftover cake seems a stretch. But going without dessert also seems the height of unfairness. So we'll compromise: Store-bought muffin makes this sinfully delicious dessert delightfully easy.

If lemon poppy seed isn't available, the combinations are limited only by your imagination. Try angel food cake with kirsch and strawberries. Chocolate pound cake with orange marmalade and almonds. Spice cake with blackberries and ginger cookies. Or whatever else occurs to you and your local muffin shop.

Serves 2

¼ cup heavy cream

1 teaspoon sugar

½ teaspoon bourbon or vanilla extract

1 store-bought lemon poppy seed muffin or cake

2 tablespoons blueberry jam

1 cup fresh blueberries

2 pizelle cookies, slightly crushed

1. Whisk the cream, sugar, and bourbon together in a small bowl until the cream forms soft peaks.

2. Halve the muffin. Break up one half and divide the pieces between two 1-cup mugs or ramekins.

3. Spoon the jam on top of each muffin portion, and then pour half the cream mixture over. Add half of the blueberries and half of the crushed cookies.

4. Break the remaining muffin into the ramekins and top with the remaining cream, blueberries, and cookies.

5. Refrigerate until ready to serve.

STRAWBERRY CHERRY SOUP

This taste-of-sunny-days recipe is intended as a dessert, but it could easily be a light dinner served with a salad on a hot summer day. The tang of the strawberries and cherries pairs beautifully with the richness of the yogurt and the tiny bit of sugar. I first served this dessert to friends at the end of an al fresco summer meal that went late into the evening. As the sun eased lower and lower in the sky, the candles on the table became our only light.

Serves 4 as a light dessert

¾ cup sliced strawberries

¾ cup halved and pitted black cherries

1 cup fresh orange juice

¼ cup whole-milk ricotta or Greek yogurt

1 tablespoon sugar

A few fresh mint leaves, for garnish

1. Purée the strawberries, cherries, orange juice, ricotta, and sugar with an immersion blender or in a standing blender.

2. Serve chilled, garnished with mint leaves.

BERRY AND RICOTTA PARFAIT WITH BALSAMIC GLAZE

The trick in small kitchens is about creating food that's wonderful and beautiful without a long, drawn-out process. Simple is better. Always. But that doesn't mean that elegant and delightful go out the window. To the contrary, simple requires that the few ingredients of a recipe take center stage. They must steal the show. And this recipe is a prime example of how that works. All hail beautiful berries!

Serves 2

1 cup sliced strawberries

1 cup raspberries

3 tablespoons sugar

¾ cup whole-milk ricotta

Drizzle of balsamic glaze or pomegranate molasses

Fresh mint leaves, for garnish

1. Combine the strawberries, raspberries, and 1½ tablespoons of the sugar in a small bowl, mix gently, and set aside for 30 minutes.

2. Whisk the remaining 1½ tablespoons sugar into the ricotta in a small bowl. Divide the sweetened ricotta evenly between two 1-cup Mason jars or mugs, reserving two tiny dollops for garnish.

3. Spoon the berries on top, drizzle with the glaze, and dot with the remaining ricotta. Garnish with mint leaves and serve.

CHOCOLATE TAHINI PUDDING

My friend Glen sails with us regularly and is often down in the galley in the wee early-morning hours when I'm making all the decisions about what we'll be eating for the rest of the day. I'll often share out loud what I'm thinking because I know he likes to hear the winding road of my thought process, and I like to share with him because it helps me hear what I'm thinking about. Somehow, when I put the words out into the space of the galley, I'm able to see the big picture a little more clearly.

In any event, because I'm having these "out loud" conversations, Glen gets a preview and, many times, an input. Long before he talked me into doughnuts (his favorite), he talked me into pudding.

Serves 2

1½ cups whole milk or oat milk

¼ cup sugar

2 tablespoons cornstarch

1 teaspoon vanilla extract

Pinch of kosher salt

¼ cup tahini

½ cup shaved bittersweet chocolate

¼ cup heavy cream (optional)

1 teaspoon cocoa powder (optional)

1. Whisk the milk, sugar, cornstarch, vanilla, and salt together in a small saucepan. Bring to a full boil over medium heat, whisking often to make sure the bottom doesn't scorch. When the mixture comes to a boil, remove from the heat, add the tahini, and whisk well until fully incorporated.

2. Add the chocolate and let the mixture sit, stirring occasionally, until the chocolate is melted. Transfer to two 1-cup Mason jars or mugs, cover with plastic wrap, and chill.

3. For an extra-rich dessert, whip the cream to soft peaks, dollop onto the pudding, and dust with cocoa powder. Serve cold.

STRAWBERRY AND LEMON PAVLOVA

Crème brûlée is a standard dessert in my world, which means that leftover egg whites are also standard. What to do with them was a quandary until a friend introduced me to pavlovas—light, fluffy, delicious, and ever-adaptable to whatever fruit is fresh and lovely in the moment. Two egg whites will make six pavlovas. They will keep in an airtight container for several days to snack on with afternoon coffee.

The only issue is equipment. While I've made pavlovas without an electric mixer more than once, it's definitely a workout, so if you don't have some mechanical way of beating the egg whites, maybe go for the Coconut Macaroons (page 212) instead.

Serves 2 (with 4 pavlovas left over)

PAVLOVAS
- ½ cup sugar
- ½ teaspoon cornstarch
- 2 egg whites
- ½ teaspoon vanilla extract
- ½ teaspoon distilled white vinegar
- Fresh mint leaves, for garnish

WHIPPED CREAM
- ¼ cup heavy cream
- 1 teaspoon granulated sugar
- ½ teaspoon vanilla

STRAWBERRY TOPPING
- 1 cup sliced strawberries (about 6 strawberries)
- 4 teaspoons sugar
- Squeeze of fresh lemon juice
- Freshly ground black pepper

1. Preheat the oven to 250°F (120°C).

2. To make the pavlovas, combine the sugar and cornstarch in a small bowl. Beat the egg whites with a handheld mixer in a medium bowl, 3 to 4 minutes, until the whites form soft peaks. Slowly add the sugar and cornstarch. Beat until stiff peaks have formed, another 1 to 2 minutes. Add the vanilla and vinegar and beat for another 10 seconds, just to combine.

3. Lay a piece of parchment on a baking sheet. Use a spoon to scoop the egg-white mixture onto the parchment, forming six round, evenly spaced disks. Bake for 50 to 60 minutes, until a lightly golden crust has formed. Remove from the oven and cool completely.

4. To make the whipped cream, whisk the cream, sugar, and vanilla together in a small bowl until soft peaks form. Cover and refrigerate until you're ready to use it.

5. Combine the strawberries, sugar, lemon juice, and several grinds of black pepper in a small bowl. Cover and set aside until you're ready to use them.

6. When the pavlovas are cool, top with the whipped cream and then the strawberry topping. Garnish with mint leaves.

COCONUT MACAROONS

Here's another utterly delicious way to use up leftover egg whites—and you only need two, since this recipe makes only eight cookies. That's enough to satisfy a sweet tooth for several days, but not so many that you'll have them on hand for long.

8 cookies

1½ cups unsweetened shredded coconut

2 egg whites

¼ cup sugar

½ teaspoon vanilla extract

Pinch of table salt

1. Preheat the oven to 350°F (180°C).

2. Spread the coconut on a baking sheet and toast in the oven for 3 to 5 minutes, until the coconut has just barely begun to brown.

3. Whisk the egg whites, sugar, vanilla, and salt together in a medium bowl. Add the toasted coconut and mix well.

4. Lay a piece of parchment on a baking sheet. With either a scoop or your hands, form the coconut mixture into eight even rounds, pressing firmly to keep them together, and set them on the parchment.

5. Bake for 15 to 20 minutes, until the macaroons are golden brown all over. Cool completely before serving.

CRANBERRY APPLE GRUNT

A grunt is just another member of the family of crisps, cobblers, Bettys, and buckles. While grunts can be made with one solo fruit, a combination makes this dessert a little more special. Cranberry and apple is delicious, but don't hesitate to try apple and raspberry, blueberry and plum, strawberry and peach . . . whatever is in season or on hand.

Serves 2

1   cup fresh or frozen whole cranberries

1   apple, peeled, cored, and diced (about 1 cup)

¼   cup plus 2 tablespoons sugar

½   teaspoon grated fresh ginger

½   cup fresh orange juice

½   cup all-purpose flour

¾   teaspoon baking powder

Pinch of table salt

Pinch of ground cardamom or cinnamon

1½   tablespoons unsalted butter, chilled

3   tablespoons milk

Vanilla ice cream or whipped cream, for serving (optional)

1. Combine cranberries, apple, sugar, ginger, and orange juice in a skillet or pan. Bring the fruit to a boil over medium-high heat and then reduce the heat, cover, and let simmer for 10 to 15 minutes, until the fruit is mostly soft.

2. Make the dumplings by combining the flour, baking powder, salt, and cardamom in a small bowl. Use your hands to rub the butter into the flour mixture until the mixture resembles coarse meal. Add the milk and mix until just incorporated.

3. Drop spoonfuls of the dough over the softened fruit mixture and replace the cover on the pan. Simmer for 5 to 6 minutes, until the dumplings are fully cooked. Serve warm, with ice cream or whipped cream, if desired.

Acknowledgments

Food and community are inextricably linked, and my personal community is no exception. As I reflect on those to whom I am grateful, I feel compelled to begin with all the growers and makers of food in my world. They are too numerous to mention here, but really, they deserve the most credit, because without the care and tending that goes into creating quality ingredients the recipes in this book would be less than. Thank you to the farmers, fishermen, purveyors, and creators of quality and health. May we all honor and support you continuously and fervently.

To my *Riggin* family, to whom this book is dedicated. Most of my cooking life has been spent sharing meals with you all. I wouldn't change a thing about our time together. My life is all the richer for knowing you. To E, for being you. There are not enough words to say how much I've valued sitting next to you every day for the past 18 years. To Jesse, also part of the *Riggin* family, my bonus kid with eagle eyes.

In every creation, there needs to be someone with a second set of senses to double-check, edit, and adjust. That is part of the process of creativity. To these fabulous humans, the recipe testers, who followed my recipes exactly and gave detailed comments on what they made—thank you. May we all be able to share a meal together in the future. Shelley Alex, Andree Anne Cote, Susy Ellis, Jesse Ellis, Chris Farrow-Noble, Cindy Frederick, Jane Gamble, Caris Hahn, Pam and Mark Haydt, Patricia Johns, Denise Jose, Susan Land, Betsy Maislen, Joanne Moesswilde, Angie Muhs, Chris Noble, Phileta Riley, Pinky Rines, Ellie Roberts, Amy Wilke, and Lynn Yonally.

To the most excellent Storey Publishing team. Wow. What a process and what a team! Carleen Madigan, thank you for beginnings and ideas and for the faith that this project would be successful.

Hannah Fries, your well of patience seemed never to run dry and your eye for detail never to wane. Thank you also for allowing this book to be imbued with my voice and my personality.

Carolyn Eckert, for your professionalism and direction—especially in the time of Covid!

Kristen Teig, well, I just love the story you were able to tell with the images you created. Thank you!

Catrine Kelly, I feel our connection via our food and our love of beauty. Thank you for your beautiful creations.

Index

*Page numbers in **bold** indicate photos*